Ships of the St. Clair River

Photos and Text
by
Raymond A. Bawal, Jr.

INLAND
―――――
EXPRESSIONS

Clinton Township, Michigan

Published by Inland Expressions

Inland Expressions
42211 Garfield Rd. #297
Clinton Township, MI 48038

www.inlandexpressions.com

First Edition 2008

Copyright © 2008 by Inland Expressions

All rights reserved. Except for use in a review, no part of this book may be reproduced in any manner. No photographs, scans, or any other form of reprint in any publications, PDF files, web sites, or any other electronic or written form without expressed permission from the publisher. Please do not encourage or participate in piracy of Copyrighted material only purchase authorized copies of this publication.

DISCLAIMER

The photos, and information contained within have been researched thoroughly but while the author and publisher of this book have made every effort to provide accurate information they are by no means responsible for any errors or omissions to the publication.

ISBN-13 978-0-9818157-1-8
ISBN-10 0-9818157-1-5

Printed in the United States of America

Design by Inland Expressions

TABLE OF CONTENTS

YANKCANUCK (2) 1

PATHFINDER (3) 6

CANADIAN LEADER 11

LEWIS J. KUBER 15

ALGOEAST 20

ROGER BLOUGH 24

JOHN B. AIRD 30

PAUL R. TREGURTHA 34

MARITIME TRADER 40

JOHN G. MUNSON (2) 45

ALGOWAY (2) 49

J. A. W. IGLEHART 53

ROBERT S. PIERSON (2) 58

MAUMEE 63

HALIFAX 68

AMERICAN VALOR 73

JAMES NORRIS 78

WALTER J. McCARTHY, JR. 83

CSL TADOUSSAC 88

CHARLES M. BEEGHLY 93

QUICK REFERENCE GUIDE 98

INDEX 99

Introduction

The St. Clair River begins at the base of Lake Huron at Port Huron, Michigan and continues south for approximately forty miles where it empties into Lake St. Clair. Virtually every ship to ever have sailed the Great Lakes has passed through this waterway. This began with LaSalle's Griffon, the first ship to ever sail the upper Great Lakes, to the newest ships built for Great Lakes service.

A number of communities are located on the St. Clair River and many of these had shipping operations in the past, with some still have unloading docks which are visited by ships to this day. A large amount of tanker traffic serves the oil refineries of the Sarnia, Ontario area, and the Detroit Edison Plant at St. Clair, Michigan receives numerous loads of coal every season from ships of the thousand foot class. Also situated at various points on the St. Clair River are smaller docks serving primarily in the aggregate trades.

However, most ships on the St. Clair River are actually passing through on their way to their destinations. Many are on their way downbound for unloading ports on the Detroit River, Lake Erie, Lake Ontario, or the St. Lawrence. Many others are upbound for points on Lake Huron, Lake Michigan, or Lake Superior. Also making passage through this region is a number of foreign flagged ships which gain access to the Great Lakes through the St. Lawrence Seaway. This makes the St. Clair River one of the heaviest traveled waterways on the Great Lakes.

In this volume twenty ships are included to give the reader a cross reference of current shipping operations. These ships were selected to divide American and Canadian flagged vessels evenly, at ten each.

Also, it was desired to portray a wide range of ship types, rather then include just one type, or fleet. Also attempted was to include a number of ships from different fleets, a task becoming much more difficult as shipping companies continue to be consolidated.

Steam powered vessels, once the backbone of the Great Lakes fleet, have become much less common in the past decade, and this downwards trend may well continue for the foreseeable future as older steamers are repowered, converted into barge units, or removed from service.

The histories of these ships are current as of the start of the 2008 shipping season. All of the photographs in this book are by the author.

YANKCANUCK (2)

The **YANKCANUCK (2)** was launched on January 8, 1963 by the Collingwood Shipyards at Collingwood, Ontario. It was built for the Yankcanuck Steamship Limited fleet as a diesel powered crane vessel. This vessel is able to handle a wide variety of cargoes and carry them into ports which are inaccessible or unprofitable for larger carriers. Originally it was equipped with a 35 ton traveling electric crane to load and unload cargoes independently of shore side equipment. This installation served the ship's three cargo compartments, which when combined gave the 324 foot vessel a single trip carrying capacity of 4,550 tons.

The **YANKCANUCK (2)** was placed into service primarily in the transporting of steel coils between the Algoma Steel Corporation at Sault Ste. Marie, Ontario and Windsor, Ontario. This trade route would become, and remained this vessel's main focus of operation throughout most of its career.

The **YANKCANUCK (2)** was christened on April 27, 1963 and it passed through the Soo Locks at Sault Ste. Marie on May 1, 1963. The **YANKCANUCK (2)** carried on a name which had been applied to the first vessel to be owned by the Yankcanuck fleet. This previous vessel had been scrapped during 1959 and 1960. The **YANKCANUCK (1)** was the last of the "composite" type vessels remaining on the Great Lakes dating back to 1889.

The YANCKANUCK (2) is seen downbound at Marysville, Michigan.

On December 31, 1970 the **YANKCANUCK (2)** was sold to the Algoma Steel Corporation and placed under a newly formed marine division. Since this vessel was already primarily engaged in the movement of Algoma Steel's products this transition did not seriously change this ship's trade patterns. In 1976 the **YANKCANUCK (2)** was sold to Chemco Equipment Finance Corporation to assist in funding a major improvement that Algoma was undertaking at its steel producing facility. Following this transaction the **YANKCANUCK (2)** was chartered back to Algoma Steel and the vessel remained active in their endeavors. The terms of this sale included a buy-back option for Algoma, and in 1983 this option was exercised.

Ships of the St. Clair River

*The **YANKCANUCK (2)** passes downbound on the St. Clair River with another cargo of steel coils bound for Windsor, Ontario.*

*Being built in 1963, the **YANKCANUCK (2)**'s all cabins aft design, while not unique, was somewhat uncommon for Great Lakes ships of the time period.*

In 1991 the **YANKCANCUK (2)** was purchased by Purvis Marine Limited of Sault Ste. Marie, Ontario, following Algoma Steel's decision to divest themselves of the vessel for financial reasons. Following this sale Purvis Marine converted the **YANKCANUCK (2)** into a barge in response to labor issues concerning this vessel's operation. In this mode the Purvis tug **ANGLIAN LADY** was commonly engaged in providing motive power for the barge's voyages. In 1993, Purvis Marine reconverted the **YANKCANUCK (2)** back into a powered motor vessel following the resolution of the before mentioned labor disagreements.

Since entering service in 1963, the **YANKCANUCK (2)** has been involved in a number of incidents. In December of 1969 the **YANKCANUCK (2)** hit bottom while transiting the Saginaw River, requiring a trip to the Collingwood Shipyards for repairs.

On June 27, 1980 this ship ran aground in the St. Clair Cutoff Channel, with another grounding in the same general area occurring on August 21, 1984. No significant damages were reported in either of these cases. On July 25, 1991, while being towed by the **ANGLIAN LADY** as a barge, and bound for Chicago with a cargo of scrap iron the **YANKCANUCK (2)** ran aground on the St. Marys River near Sweets Point. The **YANKCANUCK (2)** was released from this grounding following the lightering of some of her cargo into the Purvis barge **CHIEF WAWATAM**.

*The **YANKCANUCK (2)** is shown docked at the Purvis Marine Dock in Sault Ste. Marie, Ontario during the mid 1990s.*

Due to its type of operation the **YANKCANUCK (2)** is no stranger to unique cargos, and it has carried a wide variety of them upon the Great Lakes and up into the Canadian Arctic. Some notable cargos are as follows. On November 13, 1977 it carried a load of pig iron to the Mart Dock at Muskegon, Michigan. On November 19, 1987 the **YANKCANUCK (2)** is noted as loading a cargo of iron ore pellets at Marquette, Michigan. Finally on December 29, 1997 it arrived at Erie, Pennsylvania with a 2,000 tons of pulpwood bound for the Hamermill Plant which had been loaded at Sault Ste. Marie, Ontario. This was the first such cargo of pulpwood carried into that port in 35 years.

*The **YANKCANUCK (2)** upbound on the St. Clair River at St. Clair, Michigan during the late 1990s.*

*The **YANKCANUCK (2)** downbound at St. Clair, Michigan on December 16, 2007 in a snowstorm. The vessel is showing signs of rust, attesting to her operation on salt water during the earlier part of the year.*

When constructed this vessel's design envisioned that it could be lengthened by 50 feet without any type of performance penalty being incurred. Prior to the dissolution of the Yankcanuck fleet in 1970 a proposal for another crane vessel was presented by the Collingwood Shipyards. This vessel was to be very similar to the **YANKCANUCK (2)** and would have been slightly longer at 398 feet in length. This proposal was not be acted upon by Yankcanuck Steamship.

The original electric crane was replaced in the late 1990s by a hydraulic powered end loader. As of the 2008 shipping season the **YANKCANUCK (2)** remains in active service for Purvis Marine with activities in Great Lakes, coastal and arctic trades. With its ability to carry a wide variety of cargoes, this ship has proven itself to be very capable to operate effectively in the trade for which it was constructed.

*The **YANKCANUCK (2)**, in Algoma Steel stack markings is upbound on the St. Clair River passing Interlake's steamer **J. L. MAUTHE** during the 1980s.*

PATHFINDER (3)

The **J. L. MAUTHE** was launched on June 21, 1952 by the Great Lakes Engineering Works at River Rouge, Michigan. This ship's design was derived from the United States Steel's "AAA" class. Although the "triple A" class was a in-house designation within the Pittsburgh fleet for the **ARTHUR M. ANDERSON, PHILIP R. CLARKE,** and **CASON J. CALLAWAY** this became a commonly used term for eight vessels which entered service during 1952 and 1953 following this design. Though very similar in appearance to the original members of the "AAA" class the **MAUTHE** did have noticeably smaller after cabins.

The 647 foot **MAUTHE** was built for the Interlake Steamship Company, and was constructed for the transportation of raw materials from the loading docks of the upper lakes to the steel mills of the lower lakes. On April 4, 1953 the **J. L. MAUTHE** loaded her initial cargo of 16,638 gross tons of iron ore at Duluth, Minnesota. At the time of her commissioning the **MAUTHE** was the second new vessel to be added to Interlake fleet following the Second World War, the first being the **ELTON HOYT 2nd**. Propulsion was provided by a steam turbine capable of generating 7,700 shaft horsepower, which was fed by two oil fired water tube boilers.

The J. L. MAUTHE is shown upbound at Port Huron, Michigan in the mid-1990s. By this time she was one of a few straight deck bulk carriers remaining active in the American Great Lakes fleet.

From the early 1950s and up to the late 1970s the **MAUTHE** remained to be utilized in the iron ore trade. By the late 1970s and into the early 1980s several of this vessel's class were either lengthened, converted into self-unloaders or both. However the **J. L. MAUTHE** was not modified, thus becoming the only member of this class not to be rebuilt during this time frame. As the primary mode of iron ore transportation for American markets switched to the usage of self-unloaders and 1,000 foot superships, the **MAUTHE** began to be utilized more and more in the grain trade between the upper lakes and Buffalo, New York. The grain trade began to be such a significant part of this ship's operations that by the mid 1980s it had become the **MAUTHE**'s primary cargo.

Ships of the St. Clair River

*The **J. L. MAUTHE** is seen downbound at Port Huron on a Summer day bound for Buffalo, New York with another cargo of grain.*

*The steamer **J. L. MAUTHE** enters Lake Huron, without cargo, on its way back to Lake Superior. Of note in this picture is the smaller after cabins compared to other ships of her class.*

On May 5, 1969 the **J. L. MAUTHE** struck bottom on St. Marys River suffering significant damages. Later, on December 12, 1977, while transiting the St. Lawrence River the **MAUTHE** grounded near Three Rivers, Quebec. Damages in this incident were less severe and the **MAUTHE** was able to operate for the balance of the season, with repairs being completed in early 1978. On November 12, 1980 this steamer loss steering and collided with the Great Lakes Steel dock at Ecorse, Michigan. This occurred while the vessel was upbound on the Detroit River with the **MAUTHE** receiving a four foot gash in her portside hull five feet below the waterline. Following this incident repairs were made at the Nicholson yard.

While grain had become the primary cargo of the **MAUTHE** by the mid-1980s, she did occasionally carry a cargo of ore from the upper lakes to the lower lakes. For example, in 1988 she made a couple of trips with taconite pellets into the C&P ore dock at Cleveland, Ohio where she was unloaded by Hullet machines.

The forward cabins of the J. L. MAUTHE were representive to the era in which she was built. The forward placement of the pilot house enabled the crew to have the best possible vantage point in foggy conditions along the many narrow confines of the Great Lakes. This style of design would lose favor after the 1960s, and by the mid-1970s all new lake freighters were being built with an all cabins aft design.

The last cargo carried by the **J. L. MAUTHE** as a gearless straight deck bulk carrier was actually a rare seaway cargo for this vessel in June of 1993. The **MAUTHE** loaded a split cargo of grain with part of the load being taken on at the Burdick Elevator in Huron, Ohio and the balance being loaded at the Anderson Elevator at Toledo, Ohio. This load was destined for Montreal, and following this trip the **MAUTHE** went into what was at the time considered a temporary lay-up at Superior, Wisconsin.

This lay-up became long term and the **MAUTHE** remained idle as the demand for domestic grain carriage did not justify a return to service. While this could have been the end of this ship's career, the **MAUTHE** was given a new lease on life when Interlake decided to have the vessel converted into a self-unloading barge to operate in the stone trade.

On December 31, 1996 the **MAUTHE** was towed out of her lay-up berth amid heavy ice conditions to begin her voyage to Sturgeon Bay, Wisconsin at which she arrived on January 7, 1997 under tow of the tug **JOHN PURVIS**.

While at the Bay Shipbuilding Corporation the **MAUTHE**'s power plant was removed along with the cabins which would no longer be needed. Also done during this 13 million dollar project was a conversion into a self-unloader. In early 1998 this ship returned to service following being renamed **PATHFINDER (3)**.

Today, the **PATHFINDER (3)** remains in service with motive power being supplied by the tug **DOROTHY ANN**. Since its conversion this ship has seen a variety of cargoes and ports in which it had not been active in as a straight deck bulk carrier. As of the 2008 season this barge conversion is the only one to have been undertaken by Interlake.

Ships of the St. Clair River

*The **J. L. MAUTHE** steams upbound past Marine City, Michigan in 1990.*

*The **PATHFINDER (3)** is found at the Shell Fuel Dock at Sarnia, Ontario on a Summer evening in 2000. This view illustrates the visual changes made during the conversion into a self-unloading barge.*

*A stern view of the **PATHFINDER (3)** downbound at Port Huron, Michigan on April 2, 2006 gives good view of the tug **DOROTHY ANN**.*

*The **PATHFINDER (3)** downbound at Marysville, Michigan with a stone cargo during the 2007 season.*

CANADIAN LEADER

The **CANADIAN LEADER** was built as the **FEUX-FOLLETS** by the Collingwood Shipyards at Collingwood, Ontario in 1967. It was launched on June 16th of that year and was built for the Papachristidis fleet. The **FEUX-FOLLETS** was a standard maximum seaway sized vessel of the day with a length of 730 feet, beam of 75 feet, and depth of 39 feet 8 inches. These dimensions give this steamer a carrying capacity of 28,300 tons. On October 12, 1967 this ship departed Collingwood, Ontario bound for Port Arthur, Ontario for a load of grain bound for Montreal.

Service in the Papachristidis fleet continued until that fleet was sold on March 16, 1972 and this ship became part of the Upper Lakes fleet. Following this transaction the **FEUX-FOLLETS** was renamed the **CANADIAN LEADER**. The main trade route for this ship had been the carriage of grain from the upper lakes down the seaway with a return load of ore, and after becoming part of the Upper Lakes fleet this pattern continued.

The CANADIAN LEADER is shown downbound at Port Huron, Michigan in the early 1990s with a grain cargo bound for a St. Lawrence River port.

The **CANADIAN LEADER** is one of a dwindling number of steamers still in operation on the Great Lakes under the Canadian flag. In recent years a number of Canadian straight deck bulk carriers have been removed from service and scrapped as a good portion of the grain trade patterns have shifted away from the Great Lakes, thus creating excess capacity.

This vessel is propelled by a 9,900 shaft horsepower Canadian General Electric steam turbine which enables a speed of 16.5 knots. The **CANADIAN LEADER** is very close in appearance to that of fleet mate the **CANADIAN PROVIDER**, which also operates in similar trade routes.

Ships of the St. Clair River

The graceful lines of the CANADIAN LEADER are apparent in this view as she passes downbound at Port Huron, Michigan

*The **CANADIAN LEADER** makes an early evening passage down the St. Clair River at St. Clair, Michigan during the Summer of 2000.*

Since entering service this ship has been involved in a number of incidents. On August 2, 1972 the **CANADIAN LEADER** suffered bow damage at Thunder Bay, Ontario when she struck the dock at Saskatchewan Pool #4.

On April 5, 1989 this ship was damaged after being pushed by heavy ice into the Peavey Elevator at Superior, Wisconsin. Damages were reported to the bow on the starboard side, necessitating repairs by the Fraser Shipyards after shifting over to the Port Terminal Dock at Duluth, Minnesota.

On August 21, 1998 the **CANADIAN LEADER** ran aground in the lower St. Marys River near Drummond Island while downbound with a grain cargo from Thunder Bay, Ontario bound for Baie Comeau, Quebec. This ship remained grounded until finally being released on August 23rd with the assistance of the tugs **WILFRED M. COHEN, AVENGER IV, NANCY K.**, and **ANGLIAN LADY**. After temporary repairs were made, the **CANADIAN LEADER** was rerouted to unload her cargo at Montreal, Quebec after which she went to the Port Weller Dry Docks for repairs, where she arrived on August 30, 1998.

Another less serious grounding occurred on December 2, 1999 at Duluth, Minnesota. In this case the **CANADIAN LEADER**, while requiring tug assistance, was released quickly with no damages being reported.

On September 26, 2005 the **CANADIAN LEADER** ran aground on the St. Lawrence River while upbound for Hamilton, Ontario with a cargo of iron ore from Pointe Noire, Quebec. This incident was caused by an engine failure and the vessel was released two days later with hull damages. Following unloading her cargo of ore at Hamilton the **CANADIAN LEADER** was repaired at the Port Weller Dry Docks.

The **CANADIAN LEADER** is also noted to have carried a few mentionable cargoes during her tenure in the Upper Lakes fleet. On November 18, 1982 this ship set a cargo record at Huron, Ohio when she loaded one million bushels of grain. Later, on September 25, 1988 this ship cleared Duluth, Minnesota with two 120 ton crusher shafts which had been loaded at the Port Terminal and welded to her deck. These shafts had originated from the Reserve Mining Company in Babbit, Minnesota and were bound for Quebec.

As of the 2008 shipping season the **CANADIAN LEADER** is in active duty for the Upper Lakes fleet. This ship has remained active in the grain, and ore trades for which it was designed, and with the growth in the demand for ore over the past few seasons there is no reason to believe that the **CANADIAN LEADER** will not continue in this capacity for the forseeable future.

*The forward cabins of the **CANADIAN LEADER** are of a common design for Canadian Ships built for the Seaway trade during the 1960s. This class of ships has had its numbers reduced in the past decade as several have been sold for scrapping. The shifting of Canada's grain transportation patterns is a significant contributor to these vessel's retirement.*

*The **CANADIAN LEADER** is shown pushing its way up the St. Clair River at Port Huron, Michigan on June 23, 2007.*

*On March 25, 2008 the **CANADIAN LEADER** is found to be upbound on the St. Clair River on its first trip of a new season. It is bound for Thunder Bay to load a cargo of wheat destined for a St. Lawrence River Port.*

LEWIS J. KUBER

In the early 1950s several shipping companies on the Great Lakes found themselves in a situation in which several of their vessels were reaching the end of their productive lives. This was accompanied by an increasing demand for the transportation of raw materials on the lakes. Therefore, several of these companies under the American flag placed orders with the various shipyards around the lakes. Soon these facilities were booked to capacity and other options needed to be explored to avoid lengthy delays in the availability of new vessels. This prompted several conversions of salt-water vessels into Great Lakes carriers, and it also prompted the building of lake carriers at shipyards outside of the Great Lakes.

In 1952, three ships which were intended to be utilized on the Great Lakes were launched by Bethlehem Steel's Shipbuilding Division at Sparrows Point, Maryland. These ships were the **JOHNSTOWN (2)**, **SPARROWS POINT**, and **ELTON HOYT 2nd**, with the former two vessels being built for the Bethlehem Steel's Great Lakes fleet and the latter being constructed for the Interlake Steamship Company.

The **SPARROWS POINT** was launched on April 18, 1952 and then towed to the American Ship Building Company's South Chicago yard via the Mississippi River and Illinois Waterway where final construction took place. On November 16, 1952 the **SPARROWS POINT** loaded her first cargo when she took on a load of iron ore at Superior, Wisconsin.

*A bow view of the **SPARROWS POINT** shows the pleasing lines of her forward cabins. This design was identical for the three ships built in this class, and made these vessels identifiable from quite a distance. In this view the **SPARROWS POINT** is riding high in the bow, without ballast and cargo.*

In 1958, Bethlehem decided to have the **SPARROWS POINT** lengthened from 626 feet to 698 feet at the American Ship Building Company's Chicago yard. Similar rebuildings were also done to the **JOHNSTOWN (2)**, and the **ELTON HOYT 2nd**, by the same yard. This ship's operations while in service with the Bethlehem fleet concentrated on the movement of iron ore from the upper lakes to Bethlehem Steel's facilities on Lake Erie, and Lake Michigan. Occasional trips up the St. Lawrence Seaway for ore were also undertaken as the conditions warranted them.

It was on one of these trips in August of 1974 when the **SPARROWS POINT** became "trapped" below the Welland Canal after her fleet mate, **STEELTON (2)**, collided with and destroyed Bridge 12 at Port Robinson, Ontario, thus closing that waterway down for two weeks. On September 1, 1976 this vessel damaged its rudder while backing away from the Messabe No. 5 ore dock at Duluth, Minnesota. Repairs were completed by the Fraser Shipyards at Superior, Wisconsin.

*The **SPARROWS POINT** is shown upbound in the St. Clair River at Marine City, Michigan in 1990. She is in her last year of operation for Bethlehem Steel.*

*Shown downbound with a load of iron ore at Marysville, Michigan during the 2000 season, the **BUCKEYE (3)** makes a morning passage, in Oglebay Norton colors.*

In December of 1977 the **SPARROWS POINT** ran aground in the Beauharnois Canal portion of the St, Lawrence Seaway suffering considerable bottom damages. Repairs were completed at Lorain, Ohio during the 1977-78 winter lay-up.

During the 1970s the Bethlehem fleet went through a period of transition with the addition of two thousand-foot vessels, the **STEWART J. CORT**, and the **LEWIS WILSON FOY**, to the fleet. Additionally, another thousand-footer, the **BURNS HARBOR**, was slated to enter service in 1980. These new vessels could carry more than 2 and 1/2 times the 21,900 tons of ore which the **SPARROWS POINT** could carry. Also, the new carriers were also of a self-unloading design and could off load their own cargoes, whereas the **SPARROWS POINT** was reliant upon shore side unloading facilities.

In 1980 the **SPARROWS POINT** was converted into a self-unloader by the Fraser Shipyards at Superior, Wisconsin. This reconstruction would extend the life of this ship as the economic downturn in the domestic steel industry during the 1980s led to the scrapping of several ships of similar age as the **SPARROWS POINT**. In fact, the **JOHNSTOWN (2),** which remained in the Bethlehem fleet during its entire career, but was not converted into a self-unloader, was sold for scrapping in 1985.

Following the self-unloading conversion the **SPARROWS POINT** was often utilized outside of Bethlehem's main trade routes. With the majority of ore hauling requirements in the fleet being handled by the trio of thousand footers, this ship was available for other cargoes. Thus, the **SPARROWS POINT** could often be found transporting cargoes into locations, such as the Saginaw River, in which it had not previously visited.

This ship has been involved in numerous grounding incidents since entering service, with another occurring on October 18, 1983 near Drummond Island which caused damages to approximately 100 feet of hull. Later, on July 16, 1987 the **SPARROWS POINT** struck the approach wall to the Poe Lock at Sault Ste. Marie, Michigan while upbound with a load of stone for Marquette, Michigan. While both the vessel and approach wall sustained damages, these were considered to be minor.

The **SPARROWS POINT** would be involved in one last grounding while part of the Bethlehem fleet and this occurred on November 30, 1989. The **SPARROWS POINT** had departed Escanaba, Michigan with a cargo of taconite bound for Chicago, Illinois and ran aground of the Door Peninsula in Lake Michigan. This incident required a trip to the Sturgeon Bay, Wisconsin for repairs by the Bay Shipbuilding Company.

By the 1990 season the Bethlehem fleet consisted of the **STEWART J. CORT, BURNS HARBOR, LEWIS WILSON FOY**, and the **SPARROWS POINT**. It was during this season that Bethlehem decided to further reduce their fleet by placing both the **LEWIS WILSON FOY**, and **SPARROWS POINT** up for sale. Oglebay Norton purchased both of these ships and placed this ship into operation in 1991 under the name of **BUCKEYE (3)**.

While in the Oglebay Norton fleet this ship remained in the ore, coal, and stone trades. A large percentage of the ore carried was loaded on Lake Superior destined for Toledo, Ohio. While laid up at Toledo, Ohio on April 2, 1991 the **BUCKEYE (3)** broke loose from her moorings and struck her fleet mate **MIDDLETOWN**. Damages to **MIDDLETOWN** amounted to three bent plates, with no damages being reported for the **BUCKEYE (3)**.

On November 27, 1997 the **BUCKEYE (3)** ran aground while downbound in St. Marys River near Pipe Island. Following lightering this ship was released with the assistance of the tugs **AVENGER IV, WILFRED M. COHEN, MAINE,** and **MISSOURI**. Following inspection, the **BUCKEYE (3)** was allowed to proceed to Ashtabula, Ohio.

In 2003 the **BUCKEYE (3)** remained idle at Toledo, Ohio and would remain tied up at that location until September of 2004 when business conditions improved to the point that her reactivation was deemed feasible. On December 20, 2004 the **BUCKEYE (3)** was anchored off of Port Inland, Michigan when heavy weather caused her to swing around onto the rocky bottom. Following this incident the vessel was allowed to proceed to Nanticoke, Ontario to unload its cargo of coal. From there it proceeded to lay-up at Toledo, Ohio arriving there on December 23, 2004.

Ships of the St. Clair River

*A stern view of the **BUCKEYE** (3) shows the classic lines of a typical 1950s era built Great Lakes Steamship.*

*The **BUCKEYE** (3) is shown downbound on the St. Marys River just about the enter the Rock Cut in the mid-1990s with a cargo of ore.*

During this timeframe Oglebay Norton was having serious financial difficulties, and it was decided to defer repairs to the fifty-two year old vessel. In 2005 Oglebay Norton sold the **BUCKEYE (3)** to Buckeye Holdings, which is an affiliate of K&K Warehousing of Menominee, Michigan. The selling price of this vessel was reported to be 4 million dollars.

On December 4, 2005 the **BUCKEYE (3)** arrived at Erie Pennsylvania under tow of the **OLIVE L. MOORE**. Here this ship was converted into a barge by the Erie Shipbuilding yard. Conversion into a barge unit involved removal of the ships forward, and aft cabins and the installation of a notch in the stern into which a tug, in this case the **OLIVE L. MOORE**, could attach to provide motive power. New dimensions for this vessel are now 616 feet 10 inches in length, 70 feet in beam, and 37 feet in depth.

This type of conversion is gaining popularity on the American side of the Great Lakes fleet as a cost savings method due to the reduction of crew sizes for such a vessel when compared with a conventional freighter of similar size. Another factor in such a conversion is the fact that the propulsion machinery on many sound ships are reaching the end of their serviceable lives and this necessitates a decision by the ship owner to either convert to a barge unit or repower with new engines.

Prior to entering service as a barge the **BUCKEYE (3)** was renamed the **LEWIS J. KUBER**. On September 13, 2006 this vessel arrived at Marblehead, Ohio to load its first cargo as a barge. Since then it has been very active in the aggregate trade with the Saginaw River region being a common unloading point.

On September 8, 2007 the tug **VICTORY** was placed into the notch of the **LEWIS J. KUBER** to replace the **OLIVE L. MOORE** for the balance of the season due to that latter tug requiring extensive gearbox work. As of the 2008 season the **LEWIS J. KUBER** is in active service, paired again with the tug **OLIVE L. MOORE**.

*The **LEWIS J. KUBER** is shown downbound at Marysville, Michigan on June 2, 2007. She is being pushed by the tug **OLIVE L. MOORE**, which is possibly one of the most heavily modified tugs on the Great Lakes.*

ALGOEAST

In the mid-1970s Texaco Canada was in need for the construction of a new tanker to meet its capacity demands on the Great Lakes and St. Lawrence River trade routes. At the time all domestic shipyards in Canada were booked with other orders and to avoid an excessive delay in obtaining new tonnage a special deferment was received from the Canadian government to enable a new ship to be constructed in a foreign shipyard. Hence, Mitsubishi Heavy Industries was contracted to build a tanker at its shipbuilding facility in Shimonoseki, Japan, with launching taking place on October 4, 1976.

Measuring 431 feet, 5 inches in length this ship entered service as **TEXACO BRAVE (2)**. Service in the Texaco fleet concentrated on its intended role of the movement of petroleum products around the Great Lakes and St. Lawrence Seaway. The **TEXACO BRAVE (2)** would have a relatively quiet career in this fleet although one accident was recorded during this time.

On February 10, 1982 this ship collided with the Quebec Bridge on the St. Lawrence River after being pushed into it by ice and tidal forces. Damages to the **TEXACO BRAVE (2)** were limited to the vessels mast and communication equipment. Following this minor incident the vessel went to Quebec City for a damage assessment.

Seen upbound in the St. Clair River in the mid-1990s the LE BRAVE is shown while under operation for QMT Navigation, Inc.

On September 1, 1986 the operation of the **TEXACO BRAVE (2)** was taken over by the Societe Sofati / Soconav fleet. On that day this ship cleared Toronto, Ontario with a new crew bound for Montreal, Quebec where it was renamed **LE BRAVE**. Operations in the Soconav fleet remained similar to those in which this ship had operated in previously. In 1993, operations for the **LE BRAVE** were assumed by QMT Navigation of Montreal. This arrangement would last until 1997 when the Soconav fleet ceased operations and this vessel was renamed **IMPERIAL ST. LAWRENCE (2)** by the Imperial Oil Company.

*The **IMPERIAL ST. LAWRENCE** (2) is shown upbound on the St. Clair River in 1997, shortly before being acquired by Algoma Tankers.*

*Shown while docked at Sarnia, Ontario the **ALGOEAST** is no stranger to this area as many of its trade routes bring it into this location.*

Service in the Imperial fleet continued until February of 1998 when this ship was acquired by the newly formed Algoma Tankers fleet. This firm would fulfill Imperial Oil's liquid transportation needs upon the Great Lakes, St. Lawrence River, and East Coast. Shortly after this transaction this ship was renamed **ALGOEAST**. Algoma lost little time in placing this vessel into operation as the **ALGOEAST** is noted as being in operation on the St. Lawrence River by February 9, 1998.

In June of 1999 Algoma announced that it had contracted to have this twenty-two year old vessel converted from a single hull tanker to a double hull tanker by the Port Weller Dry Docks. This procedure would enable this ship to continue operating as a viable unit in the tanker trade. The work done also included the upgrading of the cargo hold pumping and heating equipment. On December 20, 1999 the **ALGOEAST** arrived at Port Weller for this conversion, which was completed by April 28, 2000 when it departed the shipyard bound for Nanticoke, Ontario.

On August 10, 2000 the **ALGOEAST** departed Nanticoke with a cargo of 8,863 tons of Bunker C Oil for Sarnia, Ontario delivery. While transiting the Amherstburg Channel in the lower Detroit River this ship touched bottom suffering minor damage to its external and internal hull structure along the centerline of the vessel. A crack was also reported in the vessel's forepeak, with some water being able to enter.

The **ALGOEAST** ran aground on June 18, 2003 in the St. Lawrence River near Vercheres, Quebec. This grounding was caused by a loss of power, and following the restoration of power the **ALGOEAST** was able to free herself from the bottom after which she proceeded to Tracy, Quebec for survey.

The **ALGOEAST** continues in operation as of the 2008 season for Algoma Tankers with Sarnia, Ontario being a popular destination. She operates year round with the occasional lay up, with trips to Sault Ste. Marie, Ontario being common. With the modifications undertaken to upgrade this vessel in the early part of this century, the **ALGOEAST** should continue to actively serve its owners customers.

*The stern cabins of the **ALGOEAST** are typical for a Canadian Great Lakes tanker.*

*The **ALGOEAST** passes downbound on a icy St. Clair River at St. Clair, Michigan on March 23, 2008.*

*The 431 foot tanker **ALGOEAST** has seen over 30 years of service on the Great Lakes and St. Lawrence Seaway.*

ROGER BLOUGH

Since the late 1800s the growth of vessel size on the Great Lakes has been tied to the dimensions of the locks built at the Soo. During the 1960s, the building of the new Poe Lock at Sault Sainte Marie promised to offer the possibility of significantly larger vessels being able to operate between the raw material shipping points on the upper lakes and the lower lakes with their manufacturing centers.

It was against this backdrop that executives at United States Steel decided to contract the American Ship Building Company at Lorain, Ohio for the construction of a large self-unloader which would take advantage of the new lock. On October 26, 1967 the 20 million dollar contract was announced.

Even though the Poe Lock would allow the transit of vessels up to 1,000 feet in length with a 105 foot beam, the design committee at USS made the decision to limit the new vessel's length to 858 feet. It was felt at the time that there were some turns in the St. Marys River which would not allow the passage of a 1,000 footer, thus a more conservative approach was taken.

Since there was no drydock in Lorain at the time large enough to hold the entire vessel, this ship was built in two sections. The bow section's keel laying occurred on September 3, 1968 and was float launched on December 21st of that year. This 437 foot section was built without ballast tanks, also due to the confines of the existing drydock. Meanwhile a new drydock which would be able to hold the new class of ships was being built at the yard, with the keel laying occurring in this installation for the 421 foot stern section of this vessel on December 29, 1969. Both of these sections were joined together on July 25, 1970.

By early 1971 construction on this ship was nearing completion, with June of that year being anticipated for the maiden voyage. However, on June 24, 1971 a fire broke out in the engine room of the laker at around 10:00 AM that morning. This fire raged for several hours as firefighters fought to get it under control. At the time of the blaze, around 100 workers were on the ship and all but four escaped. These four men had been working in the ship's bottom tanks and were killed. The fire is believed to have started from oil leaking from a defective gasket that came in contact with an ignition source, such as an high intensity light.

After the flames had been extinguished it became apparent that the vessel had suffered heavy damage to her stern cabins, and machinery spaces. Also included in the extensive repair list, which approached 13 million dollars, was the replacement of the original Pielstick diesel engines. All of this would push back delivery to the USS fleet to Summer of 1972, a year later than planned.

On June 5, 1972 this ship was christened as the **ROGER BLOUGH**, and sea trials began four days later on Lake Erie. The **BLOUGH** was built for the purpose of moving taconite from the upper lakes to the United States Steel's facilities at Gary, Indiana and Conneaut, Ohio. Although United States Steel had operated self-unloading vessels, in its Bradley Steamship subsidiary, prior to the construction of this ship, the **BLOUGH** was the first ship of this type in the organization committed to the ore trade.

The **BLOUGH**, and the first thousand footer **STEWART J. CORT** were the last ships built for the American Greats Lakes fleet which were built with cabin structures both fore and aft. Of the two, the **BLOUGH** retained a more traditional layout with living quarters for crew at the bow and stern. By contrast, the **CORT** has all of its living quarters at the bow, with the stern containing engine spaces, and unloading gear.

On June 15, 1972, the **ROGER BLOUGH** departed Lorain, Ohio bound for Two Harbors, Minnesota on its maiden voyage. Upon its arrival at that destination it loaded 41,608 gross tons of taconite.

Ships of the St. Clair River

*The **ROGER BLOUGH** is downbound with a load of taconite on the St. Marys River, just about to enter the Rock Cut, during the mid 1990s.*

*The square lines of **ROGER BLOUGH**'s stern demonstrates the vessel's 105 foot width while downbound at Port Huron, Michigan on a windy day.*

The self-unloading gear on the **BLOUGH** was unique at the time of its building. Rather than having a deck mounted boom as in a conventional self-unloader, the **BLOUGH** was fitted with a shuttle boom in the stern which can extend up to 54 feet over either side of the vessel. The reasoning behind such an installation was the fact that it was intended that the vessel would only be used to carry cargo into either Gary or Conneaut and would unload its cargo into a shore mounted hopper, rather then a pile further back from the edge of the dock. This enables the **BLOUGH** to discharge taconite at a rate of 11,200 tons per hour. Although similar shuttle type booms were installed on the **STEWART J. CORT**, **EDWIN H. GOTT**, and **EDGAR B. SPEER** they never obtained wide acceptance, in fact the **GOTT** received a conventional boom in 1996.

Though its unloading system has limited this vessel's flexibility in cargo carriage, the **BLOUGH** will occasionally carry a cargo of stone into Duluth, Minnesota where it is unloaded into a special hopper fitted at the CN/DMI&R dock.

*The **ROGER BLOUGH**'s self-unloading shuttle boom is visible in this picture of the vessel's stern. The boom can be extended over either side of the ship to unload into a shore side hopper. Also of note is the design of the stack which is similar to other stacks installed on vessels which had been converted from steam to diesel during the 1960s.*

Shortly after entering service severe vibrations were noted requiring a trip back to the shipyard in July of 1972. These vibrations were found to have been caused by impeller cavitations and required modifications to the stern of the **BLOUGH** to eliminate this issue. A ruptured fuel line caused the **BLOUGH** to anchor temporarily near Mackinac Island on July 31, 1972. On September 4, 1972 while downbound on Lake Superior cracks were found in a starboard fuel tank, with repairs being completed at Gary, Indiana.

In the early 1970s the idea of Winter shipping on the Great Lakes was being championed by United States Steel. The **BLOUGH** was to be heavily involved in these operations during the early part of its career. It was during one of the winter trips when the **ROGER BLOUGH** collided with her fleet mate **PHILIP R. CLARKE** in the Straits of Mackinac on January 11, 1973. The **CLARKE**'s forward progress had been stopped by heavy ice, when the **BLOUGH** could not stop in time and ran into the stern of the **CLARKE**. The **BLOUGH** came out of the collision with a hole in her bow, requiring repairs at Sault Sainte Marie.

On October 19, 1973 the **ROGER BLOUGH** arrived at Cleveland, Ohio with a cargo of iron ore which was unloaded directly into the steamer **A. H. FERBERT**. The 639 foot **FERBERT** then took the ore to Lorain, Ohio where it was unloaded at the United States Steel plant there. This dock is located on the Black River and ships as large as the **BLOUGH** cannot reach it. This process was undertaken to demonstrate the feasibility of using larger ships of carrying ore from the upper lakes to unloading points on the lower lakes which are not accessible by the large vessels. Although an interesting exercise, this process never became a routine part of the **BLOUGH**'s operation. This idea was not completely done away with however, as a ore transshipment facility was built at Lorain, Ohio in the early 1980s at which 1000 foot vessels would arrive with ore from the upper lakes, with this cargo being reloaded into smaller vessels which carried it to ore receiving docks on the tricky Cuyahoga River at nearby Cleveland.

Ships of the St. Clair River

*The **ROGER BLOUGH** heads into Lake Huron, passing under the Blue Water Bridge in 1990 on her way to load another cargo of taconite.*

*April 14, 2008 finds the **BLOUGH** downbound on the St. Clair River at St. Clair, Michigan. Noticeable in this view is the relative narrowness of the ship's forward cabins when compared with the width of the hull.*

The **ROGER BLOUGH** was involved in the search for survivors following the sinking of the **EDMUND FITZGERALD** on November 10, 1975. The **BLOUGH** was eastbound on Lake Superior at the time and was reported to have recovered an inflatable life raft from the sunken ore carrier.

By the early 1980s the **BLOUGH** was no longer the largest ship built for the United States Steel fleet as she had been joined by both the **EDWIN H. GOTT**, and **EDGAR B. SPEER** which were both 1004 feet in length, and with newer designs each were capable of carrying nearly 30,000 more tons of ore per trip when compared to the **BLOUGH**. Also by the early 1980s the production of domestic steel in the United States was experiencing a downturn with significant drops in demand.

It was against this backdrop that **ROGER BLOUGH** arrived at Sturgeon Bay, Wisconsin on September 12, 1981 and entered a long term lay-up. This ship would remain inactive for over 6 years, finally returning to service on September 24, 1987 when she departed for Two Harbors, Minnesota to load ore for Gary, Indiana delivery. The **BLOUGH** would operate into January of 1988, loading her last cargo of the season on the 23rd at Escanaba, Michigan.

*The design of the **BLOUGH**'s cabin placement has more in common with the traditional style of Great Lakes ships with both forward and aft cabins, unlike other vessels built during the 1970s to the present which incorporate an all aft cabins design. The **BLOUGH**, and the **STEWART J. CORT** were the last American flagged lakers to be built with forward cabins, with the **BLOUGH** being the last to enter service. The last Great Lakes vessel to enter service with forward and aft cabins is the Canadian flagged **ALGOSOO** which was built in 1974.*

At the beginning of the 1990 shipping season the **ROGER BLOUGH**, along with her fleet mates, received its current paint scheme consisting of the familiar red hull, with a large gray diagonal stripe along with a smaller black stripe on its bow. On July 15, 1992 this ship arrived a the Port Terminal at Duluth with engine troubles. During repairs the back half of the **BLOUGH**'s smokestack was cut away to gain access to the engines. The stack was put back together on July 20th and by the 22nd the **BLOUGH** cleared for Two Harbors following the completion of repairs.

In heavy winds on October 9. 1994 the **BLOUGH** began to drag her anchors and grounded in a mud bank near Fighting Island on the Detroit River. Some lightering was required, with the ship being pulled free three days later with the assistance of eight tugs.

While upbound at the Soo Locks on January 1, 2001 the **ROGER BLOUGH** struck a lock pier suffering a crack in her bow. Damages were minor and the ship was allowed to continue to Duluth where repairs were completed by Fraser Shipyard's personnel.

On August 5, 2006 the **ROGER BLOUGH** lost its rudder in the lower St. Marys River near Lime Island. At the time this ship was downbound with a cargo of taconite. The stricken vessel was towed to Gary by its fleet mate **EDGAR B. SPEER** in a side-by-side manner. Upon reaching Gary the **BLOUGH** unloaded its cargo on August 12th, and then was towed to Sturgeon Bay, Wisconsin for repairs, returning to service before the end of the month.

The **ROGER BLOUGH** is powered by two Pielstick diesel engines which generate 14,200 brake horsepower. The vessel's top speed is 16.7 miles per hour. The cargo hold which is optimized for the carriage of taconite is divided into five sections. Cargo is loaded through 21 hatches which each measure 58 feet by 20 feet. The hatches are removed and reinstalled by a traveling hatch crane which rides upon rails installed on the spar deck. Carrying capacity of the **BLOUGH** is 43,900 tons of ore at a Mid-Summer draft of 27 feet 11 inches.

As of the 2008 shipping season the **ROGER BLOUGH** remains in active service supplying ore carriage between the upper and lower lakes. Though this ship was built in the 1970s, her lines reflect a throwback to traditional Great Lakes ship construction. The **BLOUGH** is part of the Great Lakes Fleet, Incorporated fleet of vessels of which there are 8 units counting this ship. This fleet was acquired by Canadian National in 2003 and is managed by Keystone Shipping of Pennsylvania.

*The **ROGER BLOUGH's** spar deck has a distinctive curved edge, visible in this photo while she is downbound at the Soo. Rather then being at the edge of the deck as in a standard Great Lakes freighter, the **BLOUGH**'s deck rails are several feet inboard.*

JOHN B. AIRD

In 1970 the Algoma Central Railway fleet consisted of 5 vessels consisting of 2 straight deckers, and 3 self-unloading units. With the exception of the 1953 built **E. B. BARBER**, all of these ships had been built during the 1960s when Algoma began replacing their older steamers. The 1970s and early 1980s would see a continued growth period for the fleet as it continued to both acquire existing ships, while also constructing new ones. By 1985 the fleet consisted of 11 self-unloaders and 4 gearless vessels for a total of 15. No less then 10 of these ships had been built since 1970.

One such vessel built during this period of expansion is the **JOHN B. AIRD**. This ship was constructed in two sections, with the aft section being built at Collingwood, Ontario while the Port Arthur Shipbuilding yard at Thunder Bay, Ontario built the forward section. The 610 foot stern section was launched on October 21, 1982 and was taken to Thunder Bay, arriving there on April 19, 1983 towed by the tugs **WILFRED M. COHEN**, and **JOHN McLEAN**. At the Port Arthur Shipyard this section was joined to the 120 foot bow section, and was christened on June 3, 1983.

The **JOHN B. AIRD** entered service on June 13, 1983 when it loaded coal at Thunder Bay bound for delivery at Nanticoke, Ontario. As of the 2008 shipping season this is the last ship built new for Great Lakes service for Algoma Central.

The **JOHN B. AIRD** was built to transport raw materials around the Great Lakes and St. Lawrence Seaway. The ship is of the standard seaway size with a 730 foot length, 75 feet 10 inches beam, and with a depth of 46 feet 6 inches. Carrying capacity is rated at 31,600 tons at mid-summer draft, and this cargo is unloaded using a 261 foot deck mounted unloading boom.

The Algoma Central Marine fleet's emblem consists of an outline of a bear upon on a white disc which is bordered by a red ring. Upon this ring is the fleet's name. This large emblem placed on both sides of the bow, along with the stack, within this fleet make these ships immediately recognizable as being operated by Algoma.

On April 1, 1985 the **JOHN B. AIRD** was logged as the first vessel of the season to transit the Soo Locks. Interestingly, she would also be the last downbound ship of the season at the locks when she cleared on January 1, 1986.

On May 31, 1985 the **AIRD** lost engine power in the St. Lawrence Seaway, forcing her to tie up at the Snell Lock.

The most serious accident to befall this vessel thus far occurred on October 16, 1990 when a fire erupted in her unloading system while loading mill scale at Inland Steel's facility located at Indiana Harbor, Indiana. The **JOHN B. AIRD** had just unloaded coal from Thunder Bay and the fire damaged 1,400 feet of conveyor belt. It took five hours to bring the blaze under control, and four firemen required treatment for smoke inhalation.

The **AIRD** departed Indiana Harbor and proceeded to Sarnia, Ontario for repairs, arriving there on October 21, 1990. On November 15, 1990 this ship departed Sarnia, Ontario following the completion of these repairs.

*The **JOHN B. AIRD** is downbound on the St. Clair River without cargo in the mid-1990s.*

*The **AIRD**'s bulbous bow is apparent in this view of the vessel in winter lay up at Point Edward, Ontario just prior to the start of the 1996 season.*

Ships of the St. Clair River

*A Summer afternoon in 1992 catches the **JOHN B. AIRD** entering Lake Huron and just passing below the span of the original Blue Water Bridge.*

Motive power is provided by two diesel engines providing a total 9,459 brake horsepower, connected to a four bladed controllable pitch propeller. The rated speed of this vessel is 13.8 miles per hour.

The **JOHN B. AIRD** is typical of Canadian Great Lakes vessels built during the 1980s. Her general appearance is similar to that of her fleet mates **ALGOBAY**, **ALGOPORT**, **ALGOWOOD**, **CAPT. HENRY JACKMAN**, and **PETER R. CRESWELL**.

As of the 2008 shipping season the **JOHN B. AIRD** is actively serving its owners needs in the movement of raw materials to various points along the Great Lakes / Seaway region.

*A close up of the **JOHN B. AIRD**'s cabins shows a layout consistent with ship's built by the Collingwood Shipyards during the late 1970's and 80s. Though the classic curves of previous generations of lakers are gone, the design is complex nonetheless.*

Ships of the St. Clair River

At dusk on April 21, 2005 the **JOHN B. AIRD** is upbound, and loaded, at St. Clair, Michigan.

The **JOHN B. AIRD** is upbound at Port Huron, Michigan on May 17, 2008.

PAUL R. TREGURTHA

On May 10, 1981 the motor vessel **WILLIAM J. DELANCEY** departed Lorain, Ohio bound for Silver Bay, Minnesota on its maiden trip. With this event, the Interlake fleet became the first fleet on the Great Lakes to operate three one-thousand footers. This vessel was similar in appearance to the previous thousand footers built for Interlake, these being the **JAMES R. BARKER**, and **MESABI MINER**. The **BARKER** had been Interlake's first supership, being commissioned in 1976, with the **MESABI MINER** entering service a year later.

With the acquisition of a major ore hauling contract being awarded to Interlake in the late 1970s, it was deemed feasible to construct another ship of the thousand foot class. The American Ship Building Company was contracted to build this ship. This firm had also constructed Interlake's previous thousand footers. This ship would however be 9 feet, six inches longer then its predecessors with a total length of 1,013 feet 6 inches.

The **DELANCEY** was built in two sections with the forward section being constructed at American Ship Building's Toledo, Ohio yard and the stern section being built at Lorain, Ohio. Following the completion of the bow section it was towed to Lorain, where it was joined to the stern section with launching occurring on February 4, 1981.

This ship was christened on April 25, 1981. The **WILLIAM J. DELANCEY** was the last ship built by the American Ship Building Company, and was the second to last thousand footer to enter service, followed only by the **COLUMBIA STAR** which sailed on its maiden voyage on May 30, 1981.

*The **WILLIAM J. DELANCEY** is shown downbound on lower Lake Huron in 1989, its last full season carrying that name.*

Ships of the St. Clair River

*The 105 foot beam of the **PAUL R. TREGURTHA** is apparent in this view of the vessel passing St. Clair, Michigan. Note the large guest quarter windows just below the ships pilot house, on its starboard side.*

*The **PAUL R. TREGURTHA** is shown unloading coal at Detroit Edison's St. Clair facility on the St. Clair River during the 2000 shipping season.*

During its early years of operation the **WILLIAM J. DELANCEY** would be primarily utilized in the movement of taconite, with Lorain being a common destination in accordance with the movement of material for Republic Steel. The ore delivered to the Lorain pellet handling facility would be brought down the lakes in one-thousand foot vessels and unloaded there to be later reloaded into smaller "river" class ships, such as the **AMERICAN REPUBLIC**, for the trip up the Cuyahoga River at nearby Cleveland, Ohio.

The **DELANCEY** was also used to haul ore into Indiana Harbor as well, with this usually being loaded at Escanaba, Michigan. In fact early in her career she set two cargo records on this trade route with 62,701 gross tons being loaded at Escanaba on July 30, 1982, and then another record being set on August 7, 1982 with the loading of 63,007 gross tons.

Starting in 1984 Interlake began hauling coal from the Midwest Energy Terminal in Superior, Wisconsin to the Detroit Edison St. Clair Power Plant on the St. Clair River. Detroit Edison had just built an additional power plant at this location and was anticipating a significant increase in the demand of coal to supply this facility. Newspaper reports of the time indicated the initial Interlake commitment was for the carriage of 1.5 million tons of coal in 1984, with 3 million tons for the subsequent years of the contract. This was significant contract for the fleet and it employed the **DELANCEY**, among others, in fulfilling the tonnage commitments.

The **WILLIAM J. DELANCEY** nearly collided with Canada Steamship Lines' **MURRAY BAY** on August 6, 1986 while exiting the Duluth Ship Canal. Strong winds were blamed for the incident which pushed the inbound **MURRAY BAY** to within 30 feet of the Interlake carrier.

On October 27, 1986 Interlake's **JAMES R. BARKER** experienced an engine room fire in southern Lake Huron just north of the Blue Water Bridge. The fire which was caused by a broken fuel line disabled the thousand-foot vessel, and the **WILLIAM J. DELANCEY** was utilized in towing the vessel in a side by side fashion to Sturgeon Bay, Wisconsin.

After loading coal at Superior, Wisconsin on November 17, 1986 this vessel ran aground in Duluth Harbor. Plans were made to off load a portion of her cargo into the **CHARLES M. BEEGHLY**, but an unexpected three inch rise in water level within the harbor enabled the **DELANCEY** to be freed from the bottom with no damages being reported.

In April of 1988 this vessel is credited with carrying the first load of western coal into Consumers Power's B. C. Cobb Power Plant at Muskegon, Michigan. The use of this type of coal proved to successful and the facility continues to receive western coal via this trade route as of 2008.

*A close-up view of the **PAUL R. TREGURTHA**'s after cabin arrangement shows the similar design philosophy of her sister ships. This design can be traced back to Interlake's first thousand-footer, the **JAMES R. BARKER**. While the **BARKER** was designed from the start to have all cabins aft, an early proposal for Interlake's first thousand footer incorporated cabins both fore and aft. Besides the **BARKER**, and the **TREGURTHA** other ships built with similar lines where the **MESABI MINER**, and **AMERICAN SPIRIT** (ex-**GEORGE A. STINSON**).*

*The 1013 foot 6 inch length of the **PAUL R. TREGURTHA** is obvious in this view of the ship while docked at St. Clair, Michigan.*

*The **PAUL R. TREGURTHA** was the last ship built in Lorain, Ohio by the American Ship Building Company when it was completed in 1981.*

In May of 1989 this ship was renamed the **PAUL R. TREGURTHA**. This renaming had no impact of the vessel's operations, which had by this time seen it being fully committed to the movement of Coal from Superior, Wisconsin to St. Clair, Michigan with a few other cargoes thrown in to round out a season.

June 30, 1990 would see the **PAUL R. TREGURTHA** striking the north pier of the Duluth Ship Canal while departing with coal. This collision, blamed on strong currents, resulted in a two foot crack in the ship's hull, and minor damage to the pier. The **TREGURTHA** had anchored in Lake Superior following the incident, but had to return to Duluth for repairs.

A more serious incident nearly occurred at Duluth on November 22, 1993. While in the process of raising Duluth's Aerial Lift Bridge for the departure of the **PAUL R. TREGURTHA**, the bridge became stuck in a partially raised position. The height at which the bridge deck became lodged was not sufficient in height to allow the passage of the thousand-foot vessel, and required the **TREGURTHA** to stop prior to striking the structure. The crew of the **TREGURTHA** were able to stop their vessel in time to prevent the after structure from contacting the bridge, but not before the bow passed below it. After stopping the **TREGURTHA** backed out of the canal and proceeded to dock at the Port Terminal dock at Duluth. Since the **TREGURTHA** was loaded down to a depth which prevented it from using the Superior Entrance in the Harbor it could not leave until the following morning when repairs were made to the bridge enabling it to be raised fully.

The **PAUL R. TREGURTHA** was the last vessel to clear the Soo Locks for the 1995 shipping season when she locked downbound on January 15, 1996.

On December 21, 1999 this vessel's troubles at Duluth continued when she ran aground in the harbor while attempting to use the Superior Entrance. As stated previously this ship normally uses the Duluth Ship Canal when departing the twin harbors due to depth restrictions, but due to the Aerial Lift Bridge being closed for repairs the **TREGURTHA** was forced to utilize the Superior Entrance. The **TREGURTHA** was able be freed from the grounding following the off loading of some cargo into the **CANADIAN ENTERPRISE**. No significant damages were reported in this incident.

The general layout of thousand foot vessels built for Great Lakes service since 1976 followed two general patterns. Those built by the American Ship Building Company, with the exception of the EDGAR B. SPEER, followed the layout pioneered by the JAMES R. BARKER, while those built by Bay Shipbuilding followed the layout incorporated into the WALTER J. McCARTHY JR., (ex–BELLE RIVER). When compared to the latter class of vessel the pilot house on the TREGURTHA is significantly narrower.

While operating in heavy ice conditions on January 7, 2001 the **PAUL R. TREGURTHA** ran aground in the St. Marys River near Light 33. The location of this incident was near the entrance to the Rock Cut, with the vessel sustaining some damages, including flooding, to the forepeak. The **TREGURTHA** was able to free itself from the stranding and was able to continue its trip to St. Clair, Michigan with repairs being undertaken by Bay Shipbuilding during its five year survey in late January 2001.

Ships of the St. Clair River

As of the 2008 shipping season the **PAUL R. TREGURTHA** continues to primarily haul coal from the Midwest Energy Resources Company dock in Superior to the Detroit Edison facilities at St. Clair. This cargo is loaded through 36 hatches on 24 foot centers, with each hatch measuring 65 feet long by 11 feet wide. The total carrying capacity of the vessel is 68,000 tons at a mid-summer draft of 30 feet 1 inch. The **TREGURTHA** off loads her cargoes utilizing a 260 foot unloading boom.

At 1,013 feet 6 inches, the **PAUL R. TREGURTHA** remains the longest ship on the Great Lakes, and thus is commonly referred to as the "Queen of the Great Lakes", a title traditionally bestowed upon the longest ship plying the inland seas. Depsite being the longest on the lakes, the carrying capacity of this ship is eclipsed by those built along the lines of the **WALTER J. McCARTHY JR.** which due to design differences and greater draft capabilities are rated to carry over 10,000 tons more cargo then the **TREGURTHA** at maximum draft. These maximum drafts are rarely loaded as they are in excess of what can be handled by a large number of cargo handling facilities, and connecting channels on the Great Lakes.

Despite being in service for nearly thirty years, the **PAUL R. TREGURTHA** should remain the longest ship on the Great Lakes for some time to come as there are no current plans to build any new ships in the near future, much less any vessels larger then those of the thousand-footer class.

*The **PAUL R. TREGURTHA** passes St. Clair, Michigan on July 10, 2005 with coal for the St. Clair Power Plant which is just barely visible at the extreme right of this picture.*

39

MARITIME TRADER

The decade of the 1960s would see an enormous upgrading within the Canadian flagged Great Lakes fleet. With the opening of the St. Lawrence Seaway in 1959, a large percentage of Canadian vessels had become obsolete. The new lock system allowed for vessels in the 730 foot range to now traverse from Lake Superior to saltwater. Since a large portion of the Canadian fleet was built to traverse the old lock system and were thus limited to a length of around 260 feet these vessels had become outmoded and many shipping companies began to construct newer ships built to the maximum size allowed by the St. Lawrence Seaway.

The Paterson fleet, which could trace its roots back to 1915, obtained 9 vessels from new construction during the 1960s. Contrary to vessel construction for the Canadian fleet at the time none of these ships were of the maximum seaway size. One of these ships was the motor vessel **MANTADOC (2)**. This ship was built by the Collingwood Shipyards and was launched on November 23, 1966. At 607 feet 9 inches this ship was intended to serve Paterson's operations that involved shorter trade routes and more confined facilities.

Entering service in April of 1967, the **MANTADOC (2)** began serving her owners in the grain trade. The **MANTADOC (2)** was similar in design to the **SIR DENYS LOWSON** which had been built at Collingwood for the Algoma Central Railway fleet in 1964.

In 1968 this vessel suffered its only significant incident of its career thus far. While transiting the St. Lawrence River on November 11, 1968 between the Beaurhois Lock and Lake St. Francis in heavy fog the **MANTADOC (2)** collided with the French saltwater vessel **FRANCOIS L. D.**. The **MANTADOC (2)** sustained very heavy damages to the port side of her bow and forward cabins. No injuries were reported and the **MANTADOC (2)** went to Davie Shipbuilding at Lauzon, Quebec for repairs.

*The **MANTADOC (2)** passes downbound at Marine City during the early 1990s.*

*The **MANTADOC (2)** makes an early season voyage down the St. Clair River at Marine City in the mid-1990s.*

*The **MANTADOC (2)** is shown arriving at the Shell Fuel Dock at Corunna, Ontario to refuel in the mid 1990s.*

Service in the Paterson fleet would continue until December 12, 2001 when the **MANTADOC (2)** arrived for lay-up at Montreal, Quebec. On March 1, 2002 this ship was sold to the Canada Steamship Lines following Paterson's decision to abandon its Great Lakes shipping operations in order to concentrate on their grain operations.

Following this transaction this vessel was renamed the **TEAKGLEN** by its new owners. CSL did not place this ship into active service and it remained laid up at Montreal. In late September of 2002, the **TEAKGLEN** departed Montreal to load wheat at Quebec City for Goderich, Ontario. This was to be a one way trip as the vessel had been chartered to Goderich Elevators, Incorporated for use as a storage vessel arriving there on October 5th.

For most ships acquired for such a use this would have been the end of their career, but this ship proved to be a survivor as events unfolded. In 2004 this ship's registered ownership had changed to Goderich Elevators, Inc. and by late that year she had been placed up for sale. In July 2005 this ship was towed out of Goderich by the tug **EVANS McKEIL** bound for Sarnia, Ontario.

The **TEAKGLEN** remained at Sarnia until September 9, 2005 when it was towed from that location by the tug **AVENGER IV** bound for Thunder Bay, Ontario. Upon arrival, this ship was drydocked for a five year survey, along with having her hull repainted in a striking blue color scheme. On September 30, 2005 this vessel was rechristened the **MARITIME TRADER**, and was placed into service for newly formed Voyageur Maritime Trading, Incorporated.

*The forward cabins of the **MANTADOC (2)** are very similar to those of the **SIR DENYS LOWSON** which was of a very similar design, being built by the same shipyard. Interestingly the **LOWSON** would later join the Paterson fleet in 1979 and became the **VANDOC (2)**. Unlike the **MANTADOC (2)**, the **VANDOC (2)** did not have a long active career with Paterson and was scrapped at Sault Ste. Marie, Ontario in 2002, after being idle for many years.*

*A close up view of the aft cabins of the **TEAKGLEN** shows the stack painted in CSL colors. Also of note is the after mast's lower half being painted yellow, with it being painted black beginning at approximately the same level as the top of the vessel's stack. This was retained from her days in the Paterson fleet.*

*The **TEAKGLEN** passes St. Clair, Michigan on October 5, 2002, bound for use a storage barge at Goderich, Ontario. This is its only trip under this name and in CSL Colors.*

*The **MARITIME TRADER** is upbound at Marine City, Michigan on November 12, 2005 shortly after entering service in Voyageur colors.*

The **MARITIME TRADER** departed Thunder Bay on October 2, 2005 with her initial cargo of wheat for Sorel, Quebec. This ship is capable of carrying 19,400 metric tons of ore, and is powered by four Fairbanks Morse diesel engines generating a total of 5,332 brake horsepower, enabling a top speed of 16.1 miles per hour.

This ship is equipped with 6 cargo holds accessed through 18 hatches each measuring 11 feet by 38 feet. The **MARITIME TRADER** is also equipped with a 600 horsepower bow thruster to assist in docking operations, and navigation of constricted waterways.

By the start of the 2007 shipping season Voyageur Marine had two other vessels in operation other then this ship, these being **VOYAGEUR INDEPENDENT**, and **VOYAGEUR PIONEER**. The former vessel was the **KINSMAN INDEPENDENT (3)** which had been retired from the United States fleet in 2002 after serving for several years in the domestic grain trade. The **VOYAGEUR PIONEER** had been built as the **SASKATCHEWAN PIONEER** at Glasgow, Scotland in 1983 and is designed to operate in a combination of Great Lakes and ocean service.

On August 27, 2007 Voyageur Marine sold the **VOYAGEUR INDEPENDENT**, and the **VOYAGEUR PIONEER** to Lower Lakes Towing. While the **MARITIME TRADER** was not sold during this transaction, Voyageur did enter into an agreement with Lower Lakes Towing to provide sufficient cargoes to keep this vessel in operation throughout the shipping season. This contract is currently effective until December 31, 2011.

The **MARITIME TRADER** is the smallest ship currently operating in the Canadian flagged fleet which is engaged exclusively in the transport of raw materials on the upper Great Lakes and St. Lawrence Seaway. Since its construction this vessel has proven to be a survivor and with the current contractual agreement in which this ship operates it should remain in active service in the immediate future.

*The **MARITIME TRADER** passes upbound at St. Clair, Michigan on May 27, 2007, bound for a load of grain on the upper lakes.*

JOHN G. MUNSON (2)

On March 7, 1951 the keel for this vessel was laid at Manitowoc Shipbuilding's yard at Manitowoc, Wisconsin. Built for United States Steel's subsidiary Bradley Transportation Line, the **JOHN G. MUNSON (2)** was to be the lead ship of three ship class which included the **JOHN J. BOLAND (3)**, and the **DETROIT EDISON (2)**. At 666 feet 3 inches this ship was to be longest self-unloader on the Great Lakes at the time of her commissioning which occurred on August 20, 1952.

The **JOHN G. MUNSON (2)** was also the last ship built specifically for the Bradley fleet. This fleet was no stranger to commissioning large self-unloaders as in 1927 it had placed the 638 foot **CARL D. BRADLEY (2)** into service

At the time of this ship's construction, self-unloading freighters in the American fleet were utilized primarily in the stone, and coal trades. But within twenty years all new ships being built for American operators were being constructed as self-unloaders. This was due in large part to the more widespread use of taconite pellets, rather then natural ores. Taconite was developed as a way to utilize lower grade ore materials in the steel making process as high grade ores began to be exhausted. Taconite pellets are able to be easily handled by self-unloading vessels with their various belt driven unloading installations, whereas natural ore was much more irregular in shape and size.

The **JOHN G. MUNSON (2)** departed Manitowoc on August 21, 1952 for Calcite, Michigan where she would take on the first of many cargoes of stone. A year later, on July 4, 1953 this ship set a record for Limestone when it loaded 21,101 tons at Calcite, this record stood until being broken by Canada Steamship Line's **MANITOULIN (5)** in 1966.

*The **JOHN G. MUNSON (2)** is upbound at Algonac, Michigan in November of 1989 in very windy conditions. The ship is still wearing the old color scheme of a greenish hull, prior to adopting the red hull, with a grey and black stripe the following season.*

Ships of the St. Clair River

*The steamer **JOHN G. MUNSON (2)** is about to pass downbound at Mission Point, just south of the Soo Locks, on a Summer evening in the mid 1990s.*

*The stylish lines of the **JOHN G. MUNSON (2)** betray her 1950s roots. The time period of the 1950s is widely regarded to have produced some of the most stylish ships to ever sail upon the Great Lakes.*

In 1966, the **JOHN G. MUNSON (2)** received a bow thruster to increase its maneuverability in tighter harbors, and to minimize the necessity of using tugs while performing docking operations.

During the early 1970s the United States Steel fleet was a driving force behind winter navigation on the Great Lakes. Several of this fleet's ships were engaged in this activity with the **JOHN G. MUNSON (2)** being one of them. This ship is noted to have opened the Soo Locks for the 1973 season when she passed upbound with coal from Conneaut, Ohio for Duluth, Minnesota.

Also during the 1970s the United States Steel had the **ARTHUR M. ANDERSON**, **PHILIP R. CLARKE**, **CASON J. CALLAWAY**, and **JOHN G. MUNSON (2)** undergo lengthening reconstructions. All four of these ships had been built during the early 1950s, and all of these conversions took place at the Fraser Shipyards in Superior, Wisconsin. At the end of the 1975 season the **MUNSON (2)** arrived at Superior were she was drydocked and a 102 foot mid-ship section was inserted to increase the length of the vessel to 768 feet 3 inches. Work also done at this time included a conversion from coal to oil fired, along with having her boilers automated.

Following this lengthening, the **JOHN G. MUNSON (2)** returned to service in 1976 as one of the longest ships operated by the USS fleet, with only the **ROGER BLOUGH** and the chartered **PRESQUE ISLE** being longer.

The **JOHN G. MUNSON (2)** is usually one of the earlier vessels to fit out at the beginning of the shipping season and as such has had a few instances in which minor ice damage has been incurred. In March of 1978 this ship sustained rudder damage in Whitefish Bay on Lake Superior which required the **USCG MACKINAW** to tow her to Sault Ste. Marie for repairs.

*A bow view of the **JOHN G. MUNSON (2)** illustrates some of the differences between this ship and the **JOHN J. BOLAND (3)**, and **DETROIT EDISON (2)**. This ship was the first of the three to be built and does not incorporate a large A-Frame structure in its self-unloading gear which the latter two vessels feature. This gives the **MUNSON**'s unloading apparatus a much more compact appearance.*

The **JOHN G. MUNSON (2)** is one of the most active ships on the Great Lakes and carries coal, ore, and stone into a variety of ports. She may be found in almost every corner of the upper lakes, in ports both large and small. In doing so she has been involved in a few incidents.

On February 2, 1983 three persons were injured on the **JOHN G. MUNSON (2)** following a fire in the vessel's machine shop. At the time of the incident the ship was laid up at Milwaukee, Wisconsin.

The **JOHN G. MUNSON (2)** struck the outer breakwall at Lorain, Ohio on March 21, 1984. In this incident the ship sustained some bow damages and lost her port anchor. The anchor was later recovered and was reinstalled by late August of 1984.

On July 29, 1990 this ship grounded while docking at Ontonagon, Michigan and went to the Fraser Shipyards in Superior for drydocking and repairs. These were completed by August 9, 1990 with the **JOHN G. MUNSON (2)** returning to service.

While arriving at the Shell fuel dock at Corunna, Ontario on November 6, 2006 the **JOHN G. MUNSON (2)** struck the dock knocking around 200 feet of the structure into the water. There were no injuries reported in the accident, but the fuel dock which is a very busy location for the refueling of passing freighters was knocked out of service for a significant period of time.

Over the years the **JOHN G. MUNSON (2)** has been continuously upgraded to maintain efficiency. In 1986 a 1,000 horsepower stern thruster was installed. In 2000, the ship's original steam whistles were replaced by electric whistles.

This ship can carry a total of 25,500 tons of cargo at mid-summer draft, the cargo hold being divided into 7 sections. The **JOHN G. MUNSON (2)** is loaded through 22 hatches, and cargo is unloaded to shore via a 250 foot unloading boom. Motive power is supplied by a General Electric steam turbine capable of generating 7,700 shaft horsepower, and gives this vessel a rated speed of 17.3 miles per hour.

As of the 2008 the **JOHN G. MUNSON (2)** is owned by Great Lakes Fleet, Incorporated and is operated by the Keystone Shipping Company. This ship has proven to be a very versatile carrier and should remain active on the Great Lakes in the carriage of raw materials.

*On April 16, 2006 the **JOHN G. MUNSON (2)** passes down the St. Clair River. During a shipping season this ship will find her way into numerous harbors carrying coal, ore, and stone. Among her ports of call are Green Bay, Gary, Conneaut, Toledo, and Duluth to name a few. She is also known to arrive in less obvious places such as Ontonagon, and Thunder Bay.*

ALGOWAY (2)

In 1964, Algoma had the 574 foot **E. B. BARBER** converted into a self-unloader at the Collinwood Shipyards. This marked this fleet's entry into such market, and it would go on to build four similar self-unloaders from the period of 1965 to 1972, with all of these vessels being built at Collingwood, Ontario.

The first of these was the **ROY A. JODREY** which entered service late in the 1965 season and was followed by the **ALGORAIL (2)** in 1968, the **AGAWA CANYON** in 1970, and the **ALGOWAY (2)** in 1972. This class of ships was not large by contemporary standards with lengths ranging from 640 feet to 650 feet. The smaller size of these vessels enabled them to serve some of the smaller facilities around the lakes, and made them handy in carrying a variety of cargoes.

The **ALGOWAY (2)** was launched on June 23, 1972 and departed on her maiden voyage on September 21st of the same year. Her initial cargo was a load of salt destined for Michipicoten, Ontario. This ship measures 650 feet in length, and can carry 24,000 tons of cargo at a mid-summer draft. These payloads can include ore, coal, or various stone products, and are off loaded by the ships unloading equipment via a 250 foot boom mounted directly behind the forward cabins.

Since entering service this ship has been a very active carrier for Algoma, making a high number of trips per season, due in part to being utilized mostly on shorter trade routes rather then long Seaway runs.

*Without cargo, the **ALGOWAY (2)** shows her relatively deep depth of 40 feet. Also seen in this picture is the arrangement of the unloader housing and the connection holding the supports which raise and lower the unloading boom. This arrangement differs slightly from that on the **ROY A. JODREY**, and **ALGORAIL (2)** which incorporated a "A-frame" structure directly behind the forward cabins. The **JODREY** was the first self-unloader to be built for the Algoma fleet and was lost in 1974 following a hard grounding on the St. Lawrence River.*

Early in her career the **ALGOWAY (2)** was a common sight arriving at the Algoma Steel Mill at Sault Sainte Marie, Ontario. In later years this ship has been known to carry a large amount of salt which is usually loaded at Goderich, Ontario. Stone is also a large percentage of this ship's total cargo carriage during the season. In these trades this ship can often be found at the various unloading docks on the Saginaw, Detroit, and St. Clair Rivers.

On June 2, 1977 the **ALGOWAY (2)** was involved in a minor collision while transiting the Welland Canal with Canada Steamship's **ST. LAWRENCE (2)**. No damages to either vessel were noted in this incident. Later in that same season this ship struck a submerged object on the St, Marys River, suffering a gash in the bow requiring repairs at the Port Weller Drydocks. The **ALGOWAY (2)** cleared Port Weller on December 9, 1977 following completion of these repairs.

*The **ALGOWAY** (2) is shown unloading stone at Sarnia, Ontario during the late 1990s.*

*The **ALGOWAY** (2) is receiving some repairs to her unloading equipment, as evidenced by the tarps covering the unloader housing, while in winter lay up at Point Edward, Ontario.*

On April 4, 1994, while upbound in Lake Huron a crack was discovered in the hull of the **ALGOWAY (2)**. At the time the vessel was on her way to Chicago, Illinois with a salt cargo which had been loaded at Goderich. This required repairs, after she had returned to Goderich to off load her cargo.

The **ALGOWAY (2)** had her aft mast bent when she was departing the Black River at Lorain, Ohio on April 1, 2000. While passing under the Norfolk & Southern Railroad bridge the bridge was lowered too quickly and struck the ship's mast, bending it by 45 degrees. The **ALGOWAY (2)** arrived at Sarnia the following day where the damaged mast was repaired.

This ship ran aground at Kingsville, Ontario on May 11, 2001 and requiring lightering into a barge before she could be released from the bottom. The incident was considered minor with no damages being noted.

The **ALGOWAY (2)** found herself aground again on August 22, 2001 while attempting to dock at a stone dock at Sombra, Ontario. Efforts to free the ship included four tugs, these being Malcom Marine's **MANITOU**, the **MENASHA** owned by Gordon Marine, and the Gaelic tugs **SHANNON**, and **ROGER STAHL**. The **ALGOWAY (2)** was freed the following day and arrived at the stone dock with tug assistance. No damages were reported to have been incurred by the **ALGOWAY (2)**.

In early January of 2003 the **ALGOWAY (2)** suffered a holed bow when she hit a dock at Meldrum Bay, Ontario. This happened as the vessel was attempting to land at the dock to load a cargo, but following the incident the **ALGOWAY (2)** departed for Owen Sound, Ontario for winter lay and repairs.

High winds were blamed on a grounding at Port Inland, Michigan which occurred on November 8, 2005. The **ALGOWAY (2)** was able to free herself from the bottom after unloading a small portion of her cargo into fleet mate **ALGORAIL (2)**.

Numerous other minor incidents have befallen this very busy ship. With her wide range of operations and harbors she visits there is little wonder that this ship has a very involved history for a comparatively young vessel. During winter lay-up the **ALGOWAY (2)** usually lays up late in the season at Sarnia, Ontario where a variety of maintenance repairs are undertaken to ensure that she will be ready for the spring thaw of the upcoming shipping season.

As of the 2008 season the **ALGOWAY (2)** is in active service around the lakes operating for Seaway Marine Transport, which is a partnership between Algoma Central Marine, and Upper Lakes Group.

*The **ALGOWAY (2)** is shown above while upbound on the St. Clair River on September 1, 2007.*

Ships of the St. Clair River

*The **ALGOWAY (2)** passes downbound on the St. Clair River at Marysville, Michigan. During a regular season she may pass through this waterway several dozen times.*

*A stern view of the **ALGOWAY (2)** shows the square design of her stern. She and the **AGAWA CANYON** both have stern designs which are curved inwards on the after part of the ship, terminating in a flat surface which connects both sides of the hull.*

J. A. W. IGLEHART

This ship was built as the **PAN-AMOCO** in 1936 by the Sun Shipbuilding & Dry Dock Company at Chester, Pennsylvania. Originally built as a tanker this vessel entered service in Pan American Petroleum & Transportation's fleet of ocean going tankers. In 1943 this ship's ownership was transferred to the American Oil Company, with a renaming to **AMOCO** occurring twelve years later in 1955.

Service in salt water continued until 1960 when the **AMOCO** was sold for scrapping to the Boston Metals Company. The 24 year old tanker survived this fate however, when it was purchased by Huron Cement for the purpose of converting the ship into a cement carrier. Following this transaction this ship was brought into the Great Lakes in late 1960 and was tied up in Sturgeon Bay, Wisconsin. Huron Cement renamed this ship **H. R. SCHEMM**, but it would never operate under this name.

The **SCHEMM** would remain at Sturgeon Bay until 1964 when it was towed to the American Ship Building Company at Chicago, Illinois for conversion into a self-unloading cement carrier. When this ship departed the ship yard the following year it had been renamed the **J. A. W. IGLEHART**, with a christening ceremony occurring on May 26, 1965.

At the time of her conversion the **IGLEHART** was touted as the largest cement carrier in the world. At 501 feet 6 inches she was definitely the largest on the lakes, and had a carrying capacity of 65,000 barrels.

The Huron Cement's fleet of ships operated mainly out of Alpena, Michigan where its vessels would load gypsum for delivery to its other facilities around the Great Lakes. Since many of these locations were situated in confined harbors none of their vessels were very large with most being in the 400 to 450 foot range.

Huron Cement had a long history of operating vessels in the cement trade, one of the earliest being the conversion of the **SAMUEL MITCHELL** into a bulk cement carrier in 1916 by Mclouth Dock Yards in Marine City, Michigan. In 1923 the fleet put into service the **JOHN W. BOARDMAN** which was the first purpose built cement carrier on the Great Lakes. This fleet was active in the carriage of cement to the growing cities of the Midwest, and where painted with a dark green color scheme until the 1960s when the hulls were repainted in a light beige color.

A bow view of the J. A. W. IGLEHART demonstrates several interesting features of the vessel. Among them, the pointed bow betrays her ocean going roots. The structure directly behind the forward cabins is the ships unloading housing and airslide boom with which she unloads her cement cargoes into a shore side receiving hopper. The absence of anchor pockets also in indicative of an salt-water vessel. Retired for scrap on salt water in 1960 this ship found a new lease on life which seen her actively serve for no less then 41 years, 25 years longer then she had originally served on the world's oceans.

Ships of the St. Clair River

*The **J. A. W. IGLEHART** is downbound on the St. Clair River at Algonac State Park with a load of cement for Detroit, Michigan in the mid 1990s.*

*The **J. A. W. IGLEHART** has always been one of the first ships to sail following winter lay-up. As such she has on occasion been the first ship to pass through the St. Clair River of the season, she would claim this title in 1995 as shown above when she entered service in March of that year after being laid up for the winter at Detroit.*

Over the years this ship has been one of the first to depart winter lay up, and in several cases was heralded as the first ship of the year to pass through the St. Clair River. Throughout its active career this ship has experienced a number of noteworthy incidents.

On April 4, 1968, the **J. A. W. IGLEHART** ran aground at Alpena requiring the assistance of the tug **AMHERSTBURGH**, with the cement carrier being refloated on April 7th. Another early season voyage caused the **IGLEHART** some problems when she suffered ice damages while transiting Lake Huron on April 12, 1972. This caused damages which were in the range of $450,000.

While upbound on the St. Marys River on April 5, 1973 bound for Duluth, Minnesota with a cargo of cement the **J. A. W. IGLEHART** struck bottom. Some water was reported to have entered the vessel, and it proceeded for survey at Sault Sainte Marie, Michigan. After receiving a temporary patch the ship was allowed to proceed to Duluth, with repairs being carried out by the Fraser Shipyards at Superior, Wisconsin.

On January 31, 1974 the **J. A. W. IGLEHART**, along with the **PAUL H. CARNAHAN** were damaged at River Rouge, Michigan when they were struck by a barge being maneuvered by Hannah fleet tugboat. A loss of power was blamed for the **IGLEHART** running aground in Hay Lake, on the St. Marys River, on July 23, 1981. This incident was of a minor nature, with the steamer continuing on its way an hour after stranding.

December 26, 1996 would see the **J. A. W. IGLEHART** running aground in Saginaw Bay. This ship had been carrying a cement cargo bound for Carrollton, Michigan. It was required to lighten some of **IGLEHART**'s cargo into fleet mate **ALPENA (2)**, to free the stranded vessel with tugboat assistance.

*The stern of the **J. A. W. IGLEHART** is full of stylish curves. Of note is the cruiser stern, the attractive stack and mast. This ship was the first in the Huron Cement fleet to be equipped with a belt conveyor and airslide boom for the unloading of cement.*

On April 18, 2000 the **J. A. W. IGLEHART** ran aground on the Detroit River. The **IGLEHART** freed herself from this bottoming, and proceeded to the Belle Isle anchorage area for evaluation. The next day while proceeding to dock at the South Dock this ship grounded again, this time suffering forepeak damages. Despite the efforts of the Great Lakes Towing Company's **WYOMING**, **VERMONT**, and **PENNSYLVANIA** this steamer remained firmly stuck. On April 20th the **IGLEHART** was finally pulled free when the three before mentioned tugs were joined by the **ROGER STAHL** of Gaelic Towing. The **J. A. W. IGLEHART** returned to the Belle Isle anchorage area, and the **ENGLISH RIVER** was brought alongside to receive a portion of the **IGLEHART**'s cargo. Following this, the **IGLEHART** was able to make the Lafarge dock and offloaded the remainder of her cement cargo. After unloading, the **IGLEHART** departed Detroit for the short trip to Toledo, Ohio where she received repairs.

*The **J. A. W. IGLEHART** is downbound on Lake Huron in late 1989. Note that while the ship is now part of Inland Lakes Transportation, signified by its emblem on the bow, the stack still has the letter "H" installed and also the "HURON CEMENT" sideboard lettering is still in place.*

*Shown on August 7, 2005 the **J. A. W. IGLEHART** is shown in in its current paint scheme. Gone is the familiar "HURON CEMENT" logo and the "H" on the stock has been replaced with an "I".*

During slack times in the demand for cement the **J. A. W. IGLEHART** would be placed into to temporary lay-up at one of its owning company's docking facilities. In 1987, the National Gypsum Company was sold to Lafarge Cement, and by 1988 the fleet of former Huron Cement boats were owned by Inland Lakes Transportation, and operated by Inland Lakes Management.

There were no name changes during this transition, and for the most part the **J. A. W. IGLEHART** continued in its established trade routes. In 1991 the **IGLEHART** was surpassed by the **ALPENA (2)** as the largest ship in the fleet. The **ALPENA (2)** was the former United States Steel steamer **LEON FRASER** which had been converted into a self-unloading cement carrier by the Fraser Shipyards.

In July of 1996 Lafarge put the barge **INTEGRITY** into service paired with the tug **JACKLYN M.**. This brought about a period of transition for the older vessels of the former Huron Cement fleet as the classic steamers **E. M. FORD**, and **S. T. CRAPO** were laid up by the end of the season as cement storage vessels. In 2006 another barge & tug unit entered service for Lafarge, this being the barge **INNOVATION**, and tug **SAMUEL de CHAMPLAIN**.

The entry of this last barge unit into service would give Lafarge enough capacity that it was possible to take the **J. A. W. IGLEHART** out of service, and replace it with a more efficient vessel. On November 5, 2006 the **IGLEHART** arrived at Duluth, Minnesota where it joined its fleet mate **J. B. FORD** as a cement storage vessel.

The **J. A. W. IGLEHART** is powered by a 4,400 shaft horsepower Deval Steam turbine which allowed this ship to reach speeds of up to 15 miles per hour. This vessel was capable of carrying up to 13,200 gross tons of cement at a mid-summer draft of 26 feet 8 inches. Additional mobility is provided by a bow thruster unit.

As of 2008 the **J. A. W. IGLEHART** remains at Duluth, Minnesota as a storage unit, and a return to service is considered to be highly unlikely. While self-powered cement carriers were never a large portion of the Great Lakes fleet, as of 2008 only the **ST. MARYS CHALLENGER**, and the **ALPENA (2)** remain in active service on under the American flag.

*The **J. A. W. IGLEHART** is shown squeezing into the MacArthur Lock at Sault Ste. Marie, Michigan in September of 1991. The cement carrier is downbound from Duluth, Minnesota bound for its homeport, Alpena, Michigan. While not visible in this photograph, the remnants of this ship's previous name, **AMOCO**, were still visible on the hull, just below its current name at the time this picture was taken.*

ROBERT S. PIERSON (2)

From the early 1970s up to the early 1980s a number of new ships would enter service for the American Great Lakes fleet. Although a large portion of these ships were built to take benefit of the Poe Lock at Sault Ste. Marie, Michigan, there remained a market in which smaller vessels were necessary. Several docking facilities, especially unloading points, are situated in constricted waterways and are unable to handle large vessels. One such place on the Great Lakes is the steel mills located up the Cuyahoga River at Cleveland, Ohio. To reach such a location, with minimum tug assistance, was one of the main reasons for which this ship was built.

This ship was built in 1974 by the American Ship Building Company at Lorain, Ohio for the Union Commerce Bank, to be operated by Oglebay Norton's Columbia Transportation Division. The **WOLVERINE (4)** was launched on September 9, 1974 and was the last of three ships built at the Lorain shipyard which were nearly identical. The other two vessels were the **WILLIAM R. ROESCH**, and **PAUL THAYER**. Another ship, the **ROGER M. KYES**, was built by American Ship Building's Toledo, Ohio yard in 1973 with a similar appearance, but larger dimensions. This ship had been built for the American Steamship Company.

Each of these ships measured 630 feet in length, 68 feet in beam, and had a depth of 36 feet 11 inches. As mentioned before these ships were built to carry cargo into more restricted areas, but were also able to economically operate in shorter haul trade routes, in particular the aggregate trade.

The **WOLVERINE (4)** departed on her maiden voyage on October 15, 1974 when it left Lorain bound for Stoneport, Michigan to load a limestone cargo destined for delivery to Huron, Ohio. This ship can carry up to 19,650 gross tons of cargo, which is loaded through 17 hatches on 24 foot centers. Each one of these hatches measures 40 feet long by 11 feet in width. Cargo is offloaded by a stern mounted 260 foot unloading boom.

This motor vessel is equipped with very large twin stacks, and it has an elliptical stern which is different than most ships built of her era. Motive power is provided by a pair of Alco diesel engines which provide a total 5,600 brake horsepower. This power plant arrangement enables a speed of 17.8 miles per hour to be obtained.

In the early part of its career this ship was very active on the upper lakes in the ore, coal, and stone trades. It is noted that on occasion this ship would pass through the Welland Canal, as she did so in September of 1977 for Picton, Ontario to load ore. While an interesting sidelight to its normal trade pattern, trips such as this were not to become a regular part of its normal operation.

On December 1, 1980 the **WOLVERINE (4)** grounded briefly in St. Marys River near Nine Mile Point. After freeing itself the ship proceeded on her trip with no damages being noted.

The **WOLVERINE (4)** ran aground on May 17, 1982 in the Detroit River near Detroit Edison's Conner Creek Power Plant. The ship would remain stranded there for two days before being released on May 19th with the assistance of two tugs.

April 27, 1993 would see this ship running aground on Surveyors Reef near Cedarville, Michigan. Another grounding occurred on April 18, 1994 when the **WOLVERINE (4)** ran aground while entering Muskegon, Michigan while loaded with limestone bound for the Verplank Dock. With assistance from the tug **MARY BETH ANDRIE**, the **WOLVERINE (4)** was released, with no damages being reported.

While transiting the Cuyahoga River at Cleveland on September 23, 2000 the **WOLVERINE (4)** struck the dock at Tiffany's Cabaret Restaurant. Damages to the dock in the incident were estimated to be between $25,000 and $50,000, with no damages being incurred by the vessel.

Ships of the St. Clair River

*The **WOLVERINE** (4) is downbound at St. Clair, Michigan on July afternoon in 1999. This vessel has always been a common sight on the St. Clair River.*

*In this view, taken from the tour boat **DUC D'ORLEANS**, in 1998 the **WOLVERINE** (4) unloads a cargo of stone at Marysville, Michigan.*

Despite having many groundings in its history, this ship has also been called on a number of occasions to assist other vessels which had found themselves stranded. On December 10, 1975 the **WOLVERINE (4)** took onboard 1,500 tons of taconite from the **PAUL THAYER** which had ran aground in the Pelee Passage while transiting Lake Erie.

When the steamer **RESERVE** ran aground in the St. Clair River on April 12, 1992 the **WOLVERINE (4)** was called in the following day to receive a portion of the stricken vessel's cargo in an effort to free it. Finally, on April 7, 1999 the **WOLVERINE (4)** came to the aid of the **ARTHUR M. ANDERSON** which had grounded while departing Rogers City, Michigan with a stone cargo. Around 6,000 tons of cargo were offloaded into the **WOLVERINE (4)**, permitting the **ANDERSON** to float free.

In October 1994 Oglebay Norton dissolved the Columbia Transportation Division and took over the operation of the **WOLVERINE (4)**. After this the stack markings were changed with the deletion of the red start with the letter "C" being removed, leaving just a brown stack with a wide yellow band in the center. In 1995, a new stylish logo was placed upon the stack.

In August 2006, the **WOLVERINE (4)**, along with fleet mates **EARL W. OGLEBAY**, and **DAVID Z. NORTON (3)** were sold to the Wisconsin and Michigan Steamship Company of Lakewood, Ohio. This was done by Oglebay Norton to fully dissolve its marine transportation operations, enabling it to concentrate on its core business.

*The **WOLVERINE (4)** is shown unloading stone at Port Huron, Michigan in the mid 1990s. This ship is a common sight along the St. Clair River, and is ideally suited to operate in the stone trade.*

*Shown in on August 27, 2007, the **WOLVERINE (4)** is in her first season under Lower Lakes Towing management. Noticeable in this view is the vessels elliptical stern design, and the large twin stacks, which have not yet received Lower Lakes markings. Also apparent is the unique placement of the pilot house extending over the end of the unloading boom.*

*The **WOLVERINE** (4) is downbound, in ice, at Marine City during the mid 1990s.*

*The **WOLVERINE** (4) is shown downbound at Marysville, Michigan on August 27, 2007. Commonly referred to as "River Class" ships, such carriers are among the most versatile on the Great Lakes carrying a variety of cargoes such as ore, stone, and coal.*

In May of 2007 the **WOLVERINE (4)** tied up at Point Edward, Ontario along with the **EARL W.**, and **DAVID Z.** following labor issues between the Wisconsin & Michigan Steamship Company and the American Maritime Officers union. The **WOLVERINE (4)** would remain idle before returning to service on August 24, 2007.

On February 14, 2008 Rand Logistics Incorporated announced that it had acquired all three vessels of the Wisconsin & Michigan Steamship through its Grand River Navigation subsidiary. The **WOLVERINE (4)** was in turn sold to Rand's Lower Lakes Towing subsidiary and was reflagged to Canadian registry, making this vessel the first ship built for the American Great Lakes fleet since the 1970s to become part of the Canadian Great Lakes fleet.

Rechristening ceremonies were held on March 22, 2008 at Sarnia, Ontario for this ship when it was renamed the **ROBERT S. PIERSON (2)**. This marked the first time in which a ship operated by Lower Lakes had been named after an individual.

The **ROBERT S. PIERSON (2)** remains active as of the 2008 shipping season in the ore, coal, and stone trades. Trips to Lake Superior are now more common then they had been in the past, as this versatile carrier serves its new owners.

The stack markings of the Lower Lakes Towing fleet are very attractive with an Indian figurehead placed upon a stylized ship's wheel. The color bands on the stack, from top to bottom, are black, white, red, and gray.

*The **ROBERT S. PIERSON (2)** is downbound at Marysville, Michigan on July 4, 2008.*

MAUMEE

This ship was built in 1929 as the **WILLIAM G. CLYDE** by the American Ship Building Company at Lorain, Ohio. It had been built for the Pittsburgh Steamship fleet and was designed to move raw materials from the upper lakes to unloading docks on the lower lakes which served its owner the United States Steel Corporation.

The **WILLIAM G. CLYDE** departed Lorain, Ohio on April 15, 1929 on its maiden voyage, bound for Duluth, Minnesota. With a length of 604 feet the **CLYDE** was one of several straight deck freighters which were in operation for Pittsburgh Steamship at the time, and she soon settled into a regular pattern of hauling iron ore to the hungry blast furnaces of United States Steel.

In 1960, it was decided by Bradley Steamship to retire the **CALCITE**, which when built in 1912 and was that firm's first vessel. To replace this ship, the **WILLIAM G. CLYDE** was transferred to Bradley Steamship and sent to Manitowoc, Wisconsin for conversion into a self-unloader. This reconstruction, performed by Manitowoc Shipbuilding included the installation of a 250 foot unloading boom. This structure was placed forward, which was common at the time, and was supported from cables running from an attachment point on the top of the conveyor housing rather then a "A" frame structure.

Before reentering service in 1961 this steamer was renamed **CALCITE II** to carry on the name of the vessel which this ship replaced. Upon returning to operation the **CALCITE II** would usually load stone products at Calcite which is located near Rogers City, Michigan for delivery to both US Steel and various other customers around the lakes.

In 1964, the **CALCITE II** received a 3,240 horsepower Nordberg Diesel engine at American Ship Building's Lorain yard. This power plant replaced the ship's original 2,200 horsepower triple expansion engine, and can provide a speed of 11.5 miles per hour. Also installed at this time was a bow thruster unit.

As with most ships engaged in the same trades the vessel has had a number of incidents in her history. One such incident occurred on August 28, 1964 when the **CALCITE II** ran aground in the St. Marys River near Big Point.

While attempting to enter Grand Haven, Michigan on April 24, 1984 the **CALCITE II** stuck the breakwall after getting caught in a freak current. Although the impact tore out a six foot section of the breakwall, there were no damages being reported by the **CALCITE II**.

On October 20, 1987 this ship was summoned to the Detroit River to receive a cargo of coal from fleet mate **GEORGE A. SLOAN** which had suffered a serious grounding accident in the Amherstburg Channel the previous day.

The 1990s would be a busy time for this ship, as she would be involved in at least four incidents. On May 2, 1991 the **CALCITE II** went aground in the Saginaw River near Cheboyganing Creek after getting caught in strong currents. With the help of the tugs **FREDERICK T. KELLERS**, and **GREGORY J. BUSH**, the **CALCITE II** was freed within a few hours with no damages.

While at anchor off of Stoneport, Michigan on July 17, 1991 the **CALCITE II** received a distress call from the vintage ketch **MALABAR VI**, which had caught fire in Lake Huron. Arriving on the scene of the fire a half hour after receiving the distress signal, the crew of the **CALCITE II** attempted to put out the flames with shipboard equipment, but were unable to prevent the sailing vessel from sinking. The crew of the **CALCITE II** were able to save the owner of **the MALABAR VI**, with the remainder of that ship's crew being rescued by the fishing tug **MOMS MONEY**.

Ships of the St. Clair River

*The **CALCITE II** is shown while docked at the Diamond Crystal Salt Dock at St. Clair, Michigan in 1992. At one time this was a common location for USS vessels to unload coal.*

*The **CALCITE II** is shown downbound in St. Clair River during the summer of 1992 at sunset.*

While transiting the Amherstburg Channel on July 14, 1993 the **CALCITE II** lost her steering and ran aground. This ship was not released from this stranding for two days, and this occurred only after lightering a portion of her cargo, and with the assistance of the tugs **STORMONT**, **PATRICIA HOEY**, and **OREGON**. After unloading its remaining cargo at the Nicholson Dock at Ecorse, Michigan the **CALCITE II** went to Toledo for repairs, which were completed by September 13, 1993.

December 11, 1997 would see another grounding occurring in the Saginaw River when this ship struck bottom near the Zilwaukee Bridge. The **CALCITE II** was freed the following day with the assistance of the tug **JOHN PURVES**.

*The **CALCITE II** is shown just after passing under the original single span of the Blue Water Bridge in the early 1990s. Built originally as a straight deck freighter, this ship began a new career as a self-unloader in 1961 which has undoubtedly prolonged the lifespan of this venerable laker.*

As the **CALCITE II** was departing Port Inland on April 19, 2000 it ran aground. It was freed the following day with tug assistance and allowed to leave for Cleveland with its cargo of limestone.

In the year 2000, the **CALCITE II** was one of the oldest active carriers on the Great Lakes, and along with the **MYRON C. TAYLOR** was the oldest in the USS Great Lakes Fleet organization. In October of 2000 it was reported that the **CALCITE II, MYRON C. TAYLOR**, and **GEORGE A. SLOAN** had been sold to the Lower Lakes Towing's United States affiliate Grand River Transportation.

The **CALCITE II** arrived at Sarnia, Ontario for lay-up on November 5, 2000 following the sale, and was soon joined there by her other two fleet mates involved in the transaction. Lower Lakes Towing has a pattern of naming their ships after rivers in which vessels of their fleet operate, and with this in mind the **CALCITE II** was renamed the **MAUMEE**.

The **MAUMEE** was formally christened on April 21, 2001 and departed Sarnia one week later on April 28th bound for Stoneport, Michigan. This ship had been repainted in the eye catching Lower Lakes Towing color scheme of a light gray hull, and white cabins. Operations after becoming owned by Grand River remained similar to those in which she had served faithfully since her conversion into a self-unloader. This has included cargoes of sand, coal, and salt..

*Shown at St. Clair, Michigan on August 17, 2005 the **MAUMEE** had just re-entered service three months previously following an extensive refit.*

*A stern view shows off the graceful curves of the **MAUMEE** as she works her way upstream at Marysville, Michigan on November 4, 2007.*

Soon after entering service as the **MAUMEE** this ship was involved in a pair of minor mishaps at Cleveland. On May 21, 2001 this ship stuck an abutment at the Columbus Street Bridge while transiting the Cuyahoga River. A month and half later, on July1, 2001 the **MAUMEE** struck several pleasure boats when her stern swung into them while they were docked at Shooters Restaurant. No injuries were reported in the incident, although it was indicated that at least two of the small boats were heavily damaged.

During the 2004 shipping season the **MAUMEE** was idle at Sarnia, Ontario in need of extensive repair work prior to resuming operation. Following extensive work at Sarnia the **MAUMEE** departed that city in mid April of 2005 bound for Bay Shipbuilding at Sturgeon Bay, Wisconsin for drydocking. While at the shipyard the **MAUMEE** received her five year inspection, and had several other structural renewals completed. This ship finally left the shipyard on May 15, 2005, and returned to service.

With the retirement of the **CALUMET (3)** late in the 2007 season, the **MAUMEE** is now the oldest operating vessel on the Great Lakes which is not operating in the cement trade. This motor vessel is capable of hauling a total 12,650 gross tons of cargo, and this is loaded through 19 hatches equipped with telescoping hatch covers.

As of the 2008 shipping season the **MAUMEE** remains active on the Great Lakes. She has provided steady service since her construction nearly 80 years previously. Time will tell how many more seasons this vintage carrier will have.

*The classic lines of a traditional Great Lakes Freighter's forward cabins are clearly apparent in this view of the **MAUMEE**. This classic ship has served nearly 80 years on the inland seas.*

HALIFAX

With opening of the St. Lawrence Seaway in 1959 several Canadian owned shipping firms began to build ships to the maximum sizes allowed by that waterway. The Hall Corporation was no exception to this trend and it had its first 730 foot vessel, **LEECLIFFE HALL**, built at Glasgow, Scotland in 1961. The second 730 footer constructed for the Hall fleet would also be the last steam powered bulk freighter built for that firm. This ship, the **FRANKCLIFFE HALL (2)**, was built by Davie Shipbuilding at Lauzon, Quebec in 1963.

This ship's naming required the renaming of the **FRANKCLIFFE HALL (1)** which was still an active carrier in the Hall fleet at the time. Renamed **NORTHCLIFFE HALL**, this carrier had been built as a canal sized freighter in 1952 and remained active in the Hall fleet until the conclusion of the 1973 season. As the **ROLAND DESGAGNES**, this ship would meet its end on May 27, 1982 when it sank following a grounding on the St. Lawrence River.

On May 26, 1963 the **FRANKCLIFFE HALL (2)** departed Lauzon, Quebec on its maiden voyage bound for Duluth, Minnesota to load grain. Following the building of this ship, the Hall fleet placed into service four additional 730 foot vessels during the 1960s. These were, in order of their construction: **LAWRENCECLIFFE HALL (2)**, **BEAVERCLIFFE HALL**, **MAPLECLIFFE HALL**, and **OTTERCLIFFE HALL**. Meanwhile, the **LEECLIFFE HALL** was lost on September 5, 1964 on the St. Lawrence River following a collision with the salt-water vessel **APOLLONIA**.

The **FRANKCLIFFE HALL (2)** was involved in a minor incident early in her career which occurred on the St. Lawrence River near Montreal. On July 13, 1966, while transiting in heavy rainstorms occurring in the area that time, this ship made contact with the British flagged freighter **GLOXINIA**, and ran aground.

Another grounding occurred on June 6, 1967 when the **FRANKCLIFFE HALL (2)** ran aground on Lake Superior two miles off of Thunder Cape, while loaded with 600,000 bushels of wheat. The stranding occurred as the ship was transiting in heavy fog, with the ship finally being released three days later. Several hull plates required replacement in dry-dock following this incident.

The 1970s would see the **FRANKCLIFFE HALL (2)** continue to operate in the grain, and ore trades. The decade would also prove to be a quiet one for this vessel at least in the form of accidents. Only one recorded incident is noted during this time period and this happened on May 20, 1973 when the **FRANKCLIFFE HALL (2)** went aground near the Snell Lock following a power failure. The ship was freed in short period of time with no significant damages being reported.

In 1979, it was announced that **FRANKCLIFFE HALL (2)** would be converted into a self-unloader by the Port Arthur Shipbuilding Company at Thunder Bay, Ontario. This conversion involved deepening the ship by 6 feet, strengthening of the hull for ice operations, and the addition of topside unloading gear, was completed during the winter lay-up of 1979-80. In appearance the addition of the unloading gear resembled that on CSL's **FRONTENAC (5)** which had been converted in 1973.

When it resumed operations, this ship was able to operate with added flexibilities in trades it had previously been unable to operate effectively. Equipped with a 250 foot unloading boom it could discharge its cargo without the need for onshore equipment. The **FRANKCLIFFE HALL (2)** began carry cargoes in the stone, coal, potash, and gypsum trades along with its established grain and ore payloads. During the 1980-81 winter lay-up the stack of this steamer was heightened significantly to correct updraft issues, giving it a unique appearance.

Ships of the St. Clair River

*The **HALIFAX** is downbound in the MacArthur Lock at Sault Ste. Marie in September 1995. Modifications to the unloading housing since 1995 are apparent when comparing this view against the stern view from 2008 on the bottom of page 71.*

*The **HALIFAX** is downbound on Lake Huron in June 1996.*

On July 1, 1983 the **FRANKCLIFFE HALL (2)** made contact with the MacArthur Lock at Sault Ste. Marie, Michigan requiring a trip to the Port Weller Dry Docks. Later, on November 19, 1986 while secured at the Snell Lock the **FRANKCLIFFE HALL (2)** was struck by the Yugoslavian freighter **SOLTA**.

During the 1980s, Halco was experiencing financial hardships and despite a reorganization the creditors eventually took control of the company's assets. During the 1987 season the **FRANKCLIFFE HALL (2)** was chartered to Canada Steamship Lines, and would be ultimately sold to them early in 1988 following the breakup of the Halco fleet.

Canada Steamship Lines renamed this ship **HALIFAX** in 1988, and it continued to trade primarily on the upper lakes, with occasional seaway runs. The first passage through the Welland Canal with its new name is recorded as happening on April 7, 1988.

*The forward cabin style of the **HALIFAX** is common for ships built for Canadian fleets during the early St. Lawrence Seaway days of the 1960s. The large white circular emblem between this ship's name and the anchor pocket is a warning symbol indicating that this ship is equipped with a bow thruster.*

The **HALIFAX** suffered an explosion and fire in her unloading tunnel while upbound on the St. Marys River on April 6, 1993 Three crewmen had been working in the tunnel at the time, with the explosion killing one, with another receiving minor injuries. The **HALIFAX** was allowed to proceed to the Carbide Dock at Sault Ste. Marie, Michigan as quickly as possible, disregarding the speed restrictions in place on the St. Marys River. Upon arrival at the Carbide Dock the **HALIFAX** got caught in the current and overshot the dock, requiring assistance from the tugs **MISSOURI**, and **AVENGER IV**. Also assisting were the United States Coast Guard cutters **KATMAI BAY**, and **MOBILE BAY**. The crew of the **HALIFAX** succeeded in putting out the fire before it spread to other parts of the vessel. After an investigation it was determined that the explosion occurred when a mist of hydraulic oil came in contact with a unprotected halogen light.

On April 9, 1993 the **HALIFAX** arrived at Thunder Bay, Ontario where she underwent repairs at the Port Arthur Shipyard, remaining there until April 28th when she cleared Thunder Bay bound for Duluth, Minnesota.

Christmas Day of 1999 would be unkind for the **HALIFAX** as she found herself aground in the St. Marys River, following a fuel system problem which caused her to lose power. The vessel was able free herself, and proceeded to the Sault Sainte Marie, Michigan where divers found an impression in the hull measuring 10 feet wide and 30 feet long.

The tugs **OHIO**, and **IOWA** were summoned to tow the **HALIFAX** into Conneaut, Ohio on July 7, 2000 when the steamer suffered an engine failure in Lake Erie. The tugs brought the **HALIFAX** into harbor where she was secured for repairs.

*The **HALIFAX** is downbound on the St. Clair River on August 12, 2008 with a load of taconite pellets loaded at Superior, Wisconsin bound for delivery to Hamilton, Ontario.*

*Noticeable in this view is the **HALIFAX**'s unique stack which was heightened following the self-unloading conversion to improve updraft issues.*

In 2002 the **HALIFAX** was to suffer two separate incidents involving fire. The first occurred during winter lay-up on March 3, 2002 at Thunder Bay when a welder's torch set off a minor fire which was contained to a small storage room. This was followed in May by a fire in an exhaust header pipe while the **HALIFAX** was on Lake Erie, and was extinguished quickly. Damages in both of these incidents were minor, with no injuries reported.

On August 6, 2004 the **HALIFAX** ran aground in the St. Clair River near Fawn Island, requiring the assistance of Great Lakes Towing's **WYOMING** to be freed. After unloading her cargo at a local stone dock the **HALIFAX** went to Sarnia for a damage survey.

The **HALIFAX** is powered by a steam turbine rated at 10,000 shaft horsepower which enables this ship to reach speeds of up to 19.6 miles per hour making her one of the fastest on the lakes. This vessel is capable of carrying a maximum of 30,100 gross tons of cargo, although on many voyages the payloads are somewhat smaller to accommodate waterway draft restrictions. Cargo is loaded through 16 hatches which are removed and re-installed by a traveling hatch crane on the vessels deck.

Although by no means the oldest Canadian flagged vessel active on the Great Lakes, the **HALIFAX** is the second oldest in the CSL fleet, her age being exceeded only by the **CEDARGLEN (2)** which dates originally back to 1959 prior to a rebuilding for Great Lakes service in 1978. However, the **HALIFAX** is the only steam powered freighter operated by CSL, and may well be the last with the current trend of retiring or repowering of older steamers.

As of the 2008 season, the **HALIFAX** remains in service operating in the ore, coal, and stone trades.

*The **HALIFAX** is upbound at St. Clair, Michigan in June of 1999. Apparent in this view is the large unloading housing just forward of the after cabins. This style of structure has been common with self-unloader conversions given to Canadian flagged lakers which had been built during the 1960s, namely the **FRONTENAC (3)**, **ALGOMARINE**, and **ALGOSTEEL (2)**.*

AMERICAN VALOR

In 1953, the Columbia Transportation fleet placed into service two new straight deck bulk carriers, these being the **ARMCO**, and **RESERVE**. The **ARMCO** was launched on January 24, 1953 by the American Ship Building Company at Lorain, Ohio, and was commissioned on June 6, 1953. This ship left Lorain on June 9, 1953 to load a cargo of iron ore at Superior, Wisconsin.

The **ARMCO** shared the same dimensions of the "AAA" class, pioneered by Pittsburgh Steamship's **PHLIP R. CLARKE**, this being 647 feet in length, 70 feet in beam, and a depth of 36 feet. This made her, and the **RESERVE** the largest ships in the Columbia Transportation fleet until 1958 when the **EDMUND FITZGERALD** entered service.

The **ARMCO** spent a good portion of her early career hauling ore from Silver Bay, Minnesota and Toledo, Ohio. By the early 1970s several American fleets were exploring the option of lengthening some of their newer units to take advantage of the new Poe Lock at Sault Sainte Marie, Michigan. In 1974, the **ARMCO** was lengthened by 120 feet at the Fraser Shipyards in Superior, Wisconsin, thus regaining the title of the longest ship in the Columbia Transportation fleet at 767 feet. The following year the **RESERVE** underwent a similar lengthening procedure and both she and the **ARMCO** remained the longest ships in the Columbia colors until the construction of the **COLUMBIA STAR** in 1981.

*The forward cabins of the **ARMCO** are clearly indicative of a 1950s designed Great Lakes steamer. With the exception of updated navigational equipment installed since her construction in 1953, the cabins are virtually unchanged. In this view the **ARMCO** is downbound at Marysville, Michigan at sunset in the late 1990s.*

In the 1970s the **ARMCO** was one of many US flagged vessels which saw service into winter during extended season operations. On January 4, 1978 the **ARMCO** was upbound in the Livingston Channel south of Detroit, Michigan following the United States Steel steamer **IRVING S. OLDS**. At the time, both ships were transiting through a path being cut in the ice by the United States Coast Guard cutter **MARIPOSA**. When the **OLDS** ran into a heavy pack of ice and ground to a halt, the **ARMCO** was unable to come to a stop in time and collided with the stern of the stopped vessel. Damages to the **ARMCO** amounted to three holes in the bow near the anchor pockets, but above the waterline. These damages required the **ARMCO** to divert to Toledo for repairs.

Ships of the St. Clair River

*The **ARMCO** is shown downbound just below the Soo Locks about to pass Mission Point in the mid-1990s.*

*Calm waters produce a pleasing sight as the **ARMCO** silently transits the St. Marys River.*

By the 1980s the emerging dominance of self-unloading equipped vessels engaged in the hauling of bulk materials on the Great Lakes caused many ship owners to once again look at modernizing some of their vessels. The lengthening of the **ARMCO** in 1974 enabled the ship to carry up to an additional 6,650 tons of ore per trip, but the ship was still reliant upon shore side unloading equipment.

At the end of the 1981 shipping season the **ARMCO** arrived at Bay Shipbuilding in Sturgeon Bay, Wisconsin for conversion into a self-unloader. This procedure was accomplished over the winter and the ship was back in service the following season. This conversion caused a loss of capacity, in terms of iron ore, of 1,300 tons, but enabled the **ARMCO** to discharge her cargo at virtually any point she could dock at. It also opened up new cargoes and destinations for the vessel to service which she had been unable to as a straight deck bulk carrier.

The self-unloading conversion has extended the life of this vessel, and increased her productivity. As the 1980s progressed the hard economic times in the steel industry caused a significant number of American flagged vessels to be laid up for extended periods of time, some of these ships would never sail again. The **ARMCO** was not immune to periods of inactivity during this period and she would be laid up periodically as conditions dictated, one of the longest being that between October 6, 1984 to October 23, 1986 when she was laid up at the Fraser Shipyards.

*A head-on shot of the **AMERICAN VALOR** shows the impressive size of this ship. Though far surpassed by the newer carriers built since the 1970s which can carry more then twice what this ship can, this class of ships were giants of their day when constructed in the 1950s. With significant upgrades including a lengthening, and self-unloading conversion this ship remains a viable and productive vessel on the Great Lakes.*

Luckily, this vessel has not been involved in any major accidents during its career, with the most significant being the before mentioned collision with the **IRVING S. OLDS**. It has over the years suffered a few bumps and scrapes, but nothing to be considered overly serious.

In June of 2006, Oglebay Norton sold this ship, along with 5 other vessels, to the American Steamship Company. Shortly after this transaction the **ARMCO** was renamed **AMERICAN VALOR**. Interestingly, this purchase brought three steamers into the American Steamship fleet which hadn't operated a steamer since 1998 when the **JOHN J. BOLAND (3)** was retired from this fleet.

For the balance of the 2006 season the **AMERICAN VALOR** was slowly repainted in American Steamship Company colors, and by the 2007 season her new color scheme was completed. Meanwhile, the **RESERVE**, which had followed a relatively parallel career to this vessel, was converted into the barge **JAMES L. KUBER**, being operated by K&K Integrated Logistics of Menominee, Michigan.

*The **ARMCO** is shown tied up at the Soo awaiting passage through the Poe Lock. After her lengthening in 1974 this ship was confined to operate only on the upper lakes, being unable to pass through the Welland Canal.*

*On September 3, 2006 the **AMERICAN VALOR** is shown just after becoming part of the American Steamship fleet, at St. Clair, Michigan.. Note the different tones of paint on the forward part of the vessel during this time, as the paint scheme is slowly changed from Oglebay Norton colors to the colors of the new operators.*

The **AMERICAN VALOR** can carry up to 25,500 gross tons of cargo at a mid-summer draft of 26 feet, 4 inches. The vessel is powered by 7,700 horsepower steam turbine, giving the ship a top speed of 19 miles per hour. The **AMERICAN VALOR** is equipped with 23 hatches placed on 24 foot centers, with each hatch measuring 46 feet long by 11 feet wide.

As of the 2008 season the **AMERICAN VALOR** is actively trading upon the upper Great Lakes. Being one of a dwindling number of steamers on the lakes, it is possible in the future that her power plant may be replaced by a diesel engine.

Apparent in this view is the placement of the deck mounted unloading housing, along with the vessel's handsome stack. The lines of the 1950s era Great Lakes vessels were much more graceful then those which followed.

*The **AMERICAN VALOR** is upbound at Port Huron, Michigan on May 6, 2007. It is in its first full season for the American Steamship Company.*

JAMES NORRIS

This ship was launched on September 10, 1951 by the Midland Shipyards, at Midland, Ontario for the Upper Lakes & St. Lawrence Transportation Company. It was the third ship launched in a class which traces its roots to the "Super" class built in American shipyards in the 1940s for the Pittsburgh Steamship Company. This class of ships, which would eventually consist of six vessels also included the **HOCHELAGA, COVERDALE, SIR JAMES DUNN, THUNDER BAY (2), GORDON C. LEITCH (1)**. Of these the **GORDON C. LEITCH (1)**, and **JAMES NORRIS** were built for Upper Lakes, while the other four units were members of the Canada Steamship Lines. This ship was also the first ship to be built for the Upper Lakes fleet, although at the time of its construction this firm had operated numerous vessels since its inception in 1932.

The **JAMES NORRIS** loaded its first cargo when it loaded wheat at Fort William, Ontario on May 14, 1952. At the time of its entry into service this ship was rated to carry a total of 645,000 bushels of wheat. This ship was placed into the ore, grain, and coal trades in its early career, and though unable to pass through the old locks on St. Lawrence River, this changed in 1959 with the opening of the St. Lawrence Seaway.

At 663 feet, 6 inches in length, the **NORRIS** was soon out classed in size as new ships began to enter the Canadian Great Lakes fleet to take advantage of the new dimensions allowed by the locks in the St. Lawrence Seaway. By 1959, the **GORDON C. LEITCH (1)**, and **JAMES NORRIS**, had been joined in the Upper Lakes fleet by the **FRANK A. SHERMAN**, and **SEAWAY QUEEEN** which were both larger than the former vessels, with the **SEAWAY QUEEN** being the longest at 717 feet, 3 inches.

In April of 1971 this vessel is noted to have sustained damage to her rudder while departing the Maple Leaf Elevator at Port Colborne, Ontario. This damage was significant enough to require a trip to the Port Weller Drydocks, with the **NORRIS** arriving there on April 24th under tow of the tug **HERBERT A.**.

A more serious incident occurred on June 27, 1978 when the **JAMES NORRIS** ran aground at Kingston, Ontario. This grounding occurred near the harbor entrance, and required the assistance of tugs from the McAllistar Towing and Salvage Company to release her from the stranding. It was determined that the **JAMES NORRIS** had suffered bottom damage in this grounding and required repairs at Port Weller, being placed into the dry dock on July 9, 1978.

By the late 1970s ships like the **JAMES NORRIS** were becoming unprofitable to operate as straight deck bulk carriers. The long haul trade route of grain from Lake Superior down the Seaway, and a return with ore for lakes Erie or Michigan had become dominated by 730 foot freighters.

It was announced in January of 1980 that Upper Lakes Shipping had contracted with the Port Weller Drydocks to convert this ship into a self-unloader at a reported cost of 4 million dollars. The conversion of ships in same class as the **JAMES NORRIS** into a self-unloader was nothing new as the **HOCHELAGA**, and **STADACONA (3)** (ex-**THUNDER BAY (2)**) had both been converted during the 1960s.

After spending the 1980-81 winter at Port Weller, the rebuilding of the **JAMES NORRIS** was completed by mid-March 1981. This vessel was now equipped with a bow mounted self-unloading boom with a length of 250 feet, enabling it to unload its cargo virtually anywhere in which it could transit. It also opened up several new ports and cargo opportunities in which this ship could now operate in, compared to the previous necessity for shore side unloading facilities.

*February 19, 1995 finds the **JAMES NORRIS** in winters quarters at Point Edward, Ontario.*

*The **JAMES NORRIS** is upbound at the St. Clair River. While the majority of this ship's operations center on Lake Ontario, it does make occasional forays into other areas of the Great Lakes.*

The first cargo carried by this vessel as a self-unloader was consigned to Clarkson, Ontario where she arrived on April 1, 1981 beginning a new phase in her career. Two years later, the **JAMES NORRIS** struck a dock while arriving at Valleyfield, Quebec on December 1, 1983 resulting in minor damages.

The **NORRIS** remained in active service for Upper Lakes until November of 1992 when she was laid up at Toronto, Ontario. The lack of cargoes for this ship lasted until May 2, 1994 when she reentered service in the aggregate trade.

The most serious accident to have occurred to the **JAMES NORRIS** thus far happened on November 12, 1995 when she sank at Colborne, Ontario after being pushed into a dock during heavy weather. Despite its age at the time of the incident, the ship was subsequently raised and received extensive repairs at Port Weller.

While entering Ludington, Michigan on October 15, 1999 the **JAMES NORRIS** ran aground, incurring damages to its forward ballast tank. Following unloading cargo the following day the **NORRIS** departed for the Pascol Shipyard at Thunder Bay, arriving there on October 19th. Repairs were completed by October 31, 1999.

*The **JAMES NORRIS** was built along the same design as that of the Pittsburgh Steamship "Super" class of the 1940s. This is highly evident in the appearance of the forward cabins of this steamer. Also visible in this view is the unloading housing placed just aft of the forward cabins. The self-unloader conversion in 1981 has enabled this ship to remain in service while all others in her class have been scrapped.*

The **JAMES NORRIS** can carry 18,600 gross tons of cargo, which is loaded into the vessel through 17 hatches. This ship is powered by a Canadian Vickers Uniflow steam engine with a 4,000 indicated horsepower rating. The engine is equipped with five cylinders, and can push the **JAMES NORRIS** at a rated speed of 16.1 miles per hour.

Though it was the largest ship in the Upper Lakes fleet when it was entered service in 1952, by the mid 1990s it was the smallest carrier in the fleet. It was also the oldest in Upper Lakes colors as this fleet had retired many of its older vessels by this time. In 1998, the **JAMES NORRIS** became the second smallest and oldest in the fleet when the **CANADIAN TRANSFER** was commissioned. This ship was created by joining the stern of the **CANADIAN EXPLORER** and the forward section of the **HAMILTON TRANSFER**, which was a "Maritime" class vessel built during World War Two as the **J. H. HILLMAN, JR.**, and had been renamed to **CRISPIN OGLEBAY (2)** in 1974 by Oglebay Norton following a self-unloading conversion. With a length of 650 feet, 6 inches the **CANADIAN TRANSFER** was thirteen feet shorter then the **JAMES NORRIS**, and since it had been launched in 1943 it was eight years younger in age.

Since the early 1990s, ULS and Algoma Central Marine have had close business ties in the operation and management of their vessels. This began in 1990 with the formation of Seaway Bulk Carriers which was an arrangement to pool the straight deck bulk freighters of both fleets to assist in more efficient operations.

*The **JAMES NORRIS** is making a turn in the St. Clair River, abreast of Marysville, Michigan, in May of 1994 so she can reach the dock to unload a stone cargo.*

*The **JAMES NORRIS** is upbound at Port Huron, Michigan on July 13, 2008.*

In 1993, Seaway Self-Unloaders was created in similar fashion with this organization focusing on the operation of the two fleet's self-unloading units. In 2000, the operations of the domestic freighters in the Upper Lakes, and Algoma fleets were taken over by a partnership between the two companies named Seaway Marine Transport, thus eliminating the earlier organizations.

During a shipping season the **JAMES NORRIS** can visit a variety of ports all around the Great Lakes. While her main trade pattern involves the clinker trade between Colborne and Clarkson on Lake Ontario. She will on occasion call on the upper lakes, and in that case she may visit ports such as Marquette, Saginaw, Bay City, Goderich, Sarnia, Grand Haven, and Drummond Island to name a few.

While operating in the stone trade on August 15, 2003 the **JAMES NORRIS** grounded in the St. Clair River near Marine City, Michigan. This stranding was not considered to be serious and the ship was able to free itself without any damages.

Despite the dwindling number of steamers in the Canadian Great Lakes fleet, Upper Lakes is in ownership of no less then five of this type of ship. Besides the **JAMES NORRIS** Upper Lakes also owns the **CANADIAN LEADER, CANADIAN PROVIDER, MONTREALAIS,** and **QUEBECOIS**.

As of the 2008 shipping season the **JAMES NORRIS** is actively serving its owners in the aggregate trades. In the Summer of that season, this ship made a number of trips into Lake Huron to load stone destined for ports on the St. Clair River. This ship has proven to be a survivor not only as being the last of her class in existence but also of having a longer career then many ships which entered service after her construction.

*The **JAMES NORRIS** enters Lake Huron on her way to Upper Lake Huron to load a stone cargo.*

*The **JAMES NORRIS** is fitted with an attractive stack reminiscent of ships built prior to the 1970s. She carries the standard ULS colors of red stack with a black band at the top, and a large white diamond placed 1/3 of the way down the stack, bisecting the placement of the black band.*

WALTER J. McCARTHY, JR.

During the 1970s, and into the early 1980s the American Steamship would carry out a program of fleet modernization which would see it place into operation no fewer then ten new ships. It was also during this time that Detroit Edison had started construction of a new power plant at their St. Clair facility located on the St. Clair River, about twenty miles south of Port Huron, Michigan. This power plant was designed to burn low sulfur coal which originates in Montana and is brought by rail to Superior, Wisconsin where it is loaded into lake freighters.

In 1976, American Steamship placed the **ST. CLAIR (2)** into operation hauling coal from Superior to St. Clair. This ship was of a unique size being 770 feet in length, and with a 92 foot beam enabling it to carry 44,000 gross tons of cargo. This ship was considered to be a step towards the building of American Steamship's first thousand footer which was to be built by the Bay Shipbuilding Corporation at Sturgeon Bay, Wisconsin.

This ship was built in two sections, with the 660 foot bow section being launched on September 30, 1976. This hull section was later drydocked where it was joined to the stern section, which had been launched on August 5, 1976. On July 12, 1977 this ship was christened , but would require dry docking before entering service after sustaining bottom damages during fit out.

Given the name **BELLE RIVER** in honor of the name of Detroit Edison's new power plant, it left Sturgeon Bay bound for Superior to load coal for St. Clair on August 31, 1977. This first cargo would total 56,073 tons with delivery occurring on September 6, 1977.

The **BELLE RIVER** was placed on a regular coal run between the Midwest Energy dock at Superior, and St. Clair, but occasionally went to other destinations as demand warranted it. On some trips this ship would off load part of her coal cargo at St. Clair, and then carry the balance to Detroit Edison's plant in Monroe, Michigan. This lightering was done to decrease the thousand footer's draft to an acceptable level to enter the docking facilities at Monroe, which is located south of Detroit.

On July 31, 1979, the **BELLE RIVER** ran into the guard gate installed on the Poe Lock at Sault Ste. Marie. Although no damage was reported to the vessel, the Poe Lock was closed for 15 hours to effect repairs.

During the 1980s, this ship remained in active service as the demand for the movement of coal continued, whereas many other ships found cargoes hard to come by as the demand for iron ore carriage declined sharply. When arriving at Detroit Edison's St. Clair facility the **BELLE RIVER** would make a 180 degree turn in the St. Clair River at Recors Point, which is a few miles north of Marine City, and dock facing upstream.

While transiting Lake Superior of November 8, 1986 the **BELLE RIVER** came to the aid of the tug **THUNDER CAPE** which had been towing the retired United States Steel steamer **B. F. AFFLECK** to the scrapyard. The **THUNDER CAPE** had encountered engine problems off of the Keweenaw Peninsula while in seas of up to twenty feet in height, forcing the tug's crew to cut the **B. F. AFFLECK** loose. The tanker **EASTERN SHELL** arrived on the scene and started towing the **THUNDER CAPE** to Thunder Bay, Ontario. When the **BELLE RIVER** arrived she helped shield the tugs from the high seas. The **THUNDER CAPE** was towed safely into Thunder Bay by the tug **PENINSULA**, after she took over the tow from the **EASTERN SHELL**. Meanwhile, the **B. F. AFFLECK** was taken under tow of the tug **AVENGER IV** arriving at the Soo on November 10, 1986.

Ships of the St. Clair River

*The motor vessel **BELLE RIVER** is upbound under the Blue Water Bridge in May of 1990 on one of its last trips under that name. By the end of that month this ship had been renamed to **WALTER J. McCARTHY, JR.**.*

*The **WALTER J. McCARTHY JR.** is unloading coal at Detroit Edison's St. Clair Power Plant at Recors Point on the St. Clair River. Serving this facility was the primary reason for which this ship was built in 1977.*

On May 25, 1990 this ship was re-christened as the **WALTER J. McCARTHY, JR.** in a ceremony at Detroit Edison's Marysville Power Plant at Marysville, Michigan. Nearly six months later, on November 4, 1990 a small fire began in the bow thruster room as the **McCARTHY** was departing the Poe Lock downbound. After tying up at the Soo for a few hours she proceeded downbound on the St. Marys River with no significant damages being noted.

This vessel came to aid of another vessel in distress on Lake Superior when it responded to distress calls from the excursion boat **GRAMPA WOO** on October 30, 1996. The **GRAMPA WOO** had been tied up at Grand Portage, Minnesota when she broke loose in high winds. The ship's captain, and first mate were onboard when she drifted into Lake Superior, which had seas running up to twelve feet in height. Since the **GRAMPA WOO**'s propellers had been removed for repairs, the 95 foot vessel could do little other then to go wherever the waves pushed her. The **WALTER J. McCARTHY, JR.** arrived and was able to get a line onto the **GRAMPA WOO**, and attempted to tow the passenger boat into a sheltered area, but this ended when the towline failed. The tugs **GLENADA**, and Canadian Coast Guard buoy tender **WESTFORT** arrived from Thunder Bay to aid in the rescue. The two crewmembers were removed from the **GRAMPA WOO** by the **GLENADA**, with the stricken vessel later running up on the rocks on Passage Island, becoming a total loss.

The design of the WALTER J. McCARTHY, JR. set the pattern of the thousand footers built by the Bay Shipbuilding Corporation. When commissioned in 1977 as the BELLE RIVER this ship became the first thousand footer to be built at Sturgeon Bay which would eventually number a total of 6 units as of 2008. While there are differences between these individual ships, they all share a common general appearance. Besides this ship, the other thousand footers built by Bay Shipbuilding include the AMERICAN CENTURY, AMERICAN INTEGRITY, INDIANA HARBOR, EDWIN H. GOTT, and BURNS HARBOR.

This ship was the first ship to pass through the Soo Locks for the 1998 shipping season when it passed downbound on March 25, 1998. In August of 2000 the **WALTER J. McCARTHY, JR.** loaded a coal cargo at Superior for delivery to Ontario Power Generation's facility at Nanticoke, Ontario. Since then this ship has become more actively engaged in the movement of western coal into this location.

The **WALTER J. McCARTHY, JR.** is also a common visitor to the Consumers Energy's Karn/Weadock Power Plant at Essexville, Michigan. This facility is located at the mouth of the Saginaw River where it empties into Saginaw Bay. While coal remains the **McCARTHY**'s primary cargo, she does on occasion carry other cargoes, with ore being the most common.

*The immense size of the **WALTER J. McCARTHY, JR.** is apparent in this view of the vessel tied up at Detroit Edison's St. Clair facility.*

*On May 8, 2006 the **WALTER J. McCARTHY, JR.** is downbound on the St. Clair River.*

While transiting the St. Marys River near Detour, Michigan upbound on September 16, 2005 the **WALTER J. McCARTHY, JR.** had a minor collision with the **ROGER BLOUGH** which was also upbound at the time. This incident occurred in foggy conditions with minor damages being suffered by both vessels.

While backing into the Hallet No. 8 dock at Superior, Wisconsin on January 14, 2008 for winter lay-up, the **WALTER J. McCARTHY, JR.** struck a submerged object tearing a 7 by 4 foot hole in the hull. This resulted in the flooding of this ship's engine room, and caused the stern to settle on the bottom in 20 feet of water. The water level in the engine room was high enough to submerge the ships four diesel engines, and salvage efforts began shortly after the accident. The **WALTER J. McCARTHY, JR.** required extensive repairs which prevented a return to service until May 6, 2008 when she loaded coal at Superior for Nanticoke.

The **WALTER J. McCARTHY, JR.** is powered by 4 General Motor Electro-Motive which create 14,400 brake horsepower. This combination provides power to the ship's twin propellers giving a rated speed of 16.1 miles per hour.

This ship can carry a total of 78,850 gross tons of cargo at a draft of 34 feet, although she is limited by the depth of the channels on her trade routes from carrying that amount of cargo. The **WALTER J. McCARTHY, JR.** is equipped with 37 hatches, placed on 24 foot centers. Cargo is offloaded by a 250 foot unloading boom. Maneuverability is enhanced with both bow and stern thruster units.

As of the 2008 season, the **WALTER J. McCARTHY, JR.** has been in active service since reentering service in May of that year following the completion of repairs undertaken following the incident at Superior.

*The **WALTER J. McCARTHY, JR.** is downbound at St. Clair, Michigan on April 7, 2007. Ice formations can be seen on the vessels bow attesting to a cold trip down the lakes.*

CSL TADOUSSAC

The 1960s would see a period of transition and growth for the Canada Steamship Lines fleet. The opening of the St. Lawrence Seaway had enabled the building of larger vessels which could operated from the upper lakes to St. Lawrence River. During this decade this fleet would retire not only its canal sized units, but also many of its older bulk carriers in favor of newer and larger vessels. By 1969, this fleet had 12 ships which were built during the 1960s in operation. All 12 of these ships were of the 730 foot class, and this vessel was to be the last ship to be built during this 1960s for Canada Steamship Lines.

The keel for this ship was laid on June 25, 1968 at the Collingwood Shipyards at Collingwood, Ontario. This ship was designed with both forward and aft cabins, and was one of the earlier vessels to be equipped with a stern mounted unloading boom with this cabin arrangement. On May 29, 1969, while in preparation for launching the **TADOUSSAC (4)** slipped from the launch way prematurely killing two shipyard workers, and injuring nearly 40.

The **TADOUSSAC (4)** departed Collingwood on October 2, 1969 bound for Fort William, Ontario on its first trip. At 730 feet in length she had been built to the maximum dimensions allowed for the St. Lawrence Seaway at the time. This ship would also be the last ship built so far for Canada Steamship Lines which had the traditional fore and aft cabin design, as all subsequent ships constructed have been with an all cabins aft design.

Early in its career, the **TADOUSSAC (4)** was involved in a couple of minor incidents. The first occurred when the this ship's unloading boom collapsed on April 25, 1973 while at Sandusky, Ohio. Another occurred on October 15, 1974 while the **TADOUSSAC (4)** was departing the DM&I Dock at Duluth, Minnesota. On this occasion this ship damaged the dock and tore off two loading spouts on the ore dock when it struck it while backing away. No significant damage was reported to have occurred to the vessel.

In 1976, ownership of the **TADOUSSAC (4)** was registered to the Power Corporation of Canada, following that firm's gaining 100 percent control of Canada Steamship in late 1975. This lasted until 1981 when ownership was taken over by the CSL Group.

Starting in the 1980s ,the **TADOUSSAC (4)** was involved in a number of mid-stream transfers of cargo into large ocean bulk carriers on the St. Lawrence River. This consisted of several lake vessels loading cargo on the lakes and hauling it up the St. Lawrence Seaway to be deposited directly into ocean ships while anchored in the St. Lawrence River. Also pioneered at this time was "topping off" service provided by ship of Canada Steamship Lines, where lakers loaded additional cargo into saltwater ships which had been loaded to maximum draft at East Coast loading facilities.

One of the first of these operations took place in early August of 1981 when this ship along with fleet mates **NANTICOKE, LOUIS R. DESMARAIS**, and **JEAN PARISIEN** collectively loaded 110,000 tons of coal, which had been loaded at Sandusky, Ohio, into a salt water bulk carrier anchored in the St. Lawrence River. Throughout the 1980s, and into the 1990s the **TADOUSSAC (4)** was involved in a number of the cargo movements. One of the largest consignments was for 150,000 tons of coal loaded at Sandusky in May of 1982 to be loaded into the **SIR ALEXANDER GLEN** at Sept Isle, Quebec. Participating in this operation besides this ship was **NANTICOKE, TARANTAU, MANITOULIN (5), JEAN PARISIEN**, and **LOUIS R. DESMARAIS**.

*The **TADOUSSAC** (4) is upbound at Port Huron, Michigan in September of 1992.*

*The **TADOUSSAC** (4) is upbound in the McArthur Lock at Sault Sainte Marie on a misty morning in the 1990s.*

While transiting the St. Clair River on April 26, 1984 the **TADOUSSAC (4)** ran aground during heavy ice conditions. At the time of this incident one of the worst ice jams in recent history was occurring delaying many vessels. She was freed two days later with tug assistance and continued downbound.

On April 2, 1990 this ship struck an abutment while passing under the Clarence Street Bridge at Port Colborne, Ontario. The **TADOUSSAC (4)** received a 11 foot crack in its hull as a result of this collision, with some damage to the bridge supports being reported.

Later that same year on November 8, 1990 this ship suffered a loss of power while returning to Whitefish Bay after trying to cross Lake Superior during heavy weather. The **TADOUSSAC (4)** experienced significant damages from excessive rolling in heavy seas until power was restored. At least one crewmember was injured in this incident, requiring him to be removed by helicopter.

This ship lost power again on April 20, 1997 near the Eisenhower Lock requiring the assistance of the tugs **ROBINSON BAY**, and **LEWIS CASTLE**. The **TADOUSSAC (4)** required repairs at Port Weller following this incident, arriving there on the 25th.

While upbound on Lake St. Clair on July 9, 1998 with coal for delivery to the Lambton Generating Station on the St. Clair River the **TADOUSSAC (4)** ran aground. Following off loading a portion of its coal cargo, the motor vessel was pulled free by the tugs **SHANNON, PATRICIA HOEY, ILLINOIS, WYOMING,** and **PENNSYLVANIA**.

The **TADOUSSAC (4)** had another run-in with a bridge abutment on September 2, 1999 when it hit one at Bridge #10 on Welland Canal. After a short delay this ship resumed full operations.

The CSL TADOUSSAC was the last ship built for Canada Steamship Lines which had a fore and aft cabin design. Of note in this picture is the wake created by the ship's enlarged hull sections at the waterline. The beginning of this wake can be seen at the extreme left side of this picture.

On November 20, 2000 the **TADOUSSAC (4)** ran aground while docking at the grain elevator at Sarnia, Ontario. It was freed the following day by the tug **MENASHA** with no damages being reported.

On December 13, 2000 the **TADOUSSAC (4)** arrived at Port Weller Drydocks where she had her cargo hold rebuilt. This reconstruction, which had been announced by CSL in March of 2000 was done at a cost of 20 million dollars. Included was the widening of the **TADOUSSAC (4)** from 75 feet in beam to 78 feet. The cargo hold was modified from a three belt into a single conveyor belt system, along with dust control equipment also being installed. Also during the reconstruction this ship's hull was repainted into an overall gray color scheme, with the cabins remaining white. The adoption of the new colors was in consideration for the cement clinker trade in which this ship was to spend a significant portion of its season operating in. On March 4, 2001 CSL rechristened this vessel **CSL TADOUSSAC**.

*The **CSL TADOUSSAC** passes upbound at St. Clair, Michigan on March 26, 2006. The "CANADA STEAMSHIP LINES" billboard lettering on the hull is barely visible due to a thin layer of ore dust left on the hull from a previous payload.*

*Clearly visible in this view of the **CSL TADOUSSAC** on June 7, 2005 is this ship's flat stern.*

In mid-June of 2001 the **CSL TADOUSSAC** returned to service for the first time in her enlarged state. Since then she has been in active service carrying a significant amount of cement clinker into the Essroc Terminal at Essexville, Michigan. She is also active in the ore trades, and this at times gives her gray hull a dark red tint from ore dust.

While in winter lay-up at Port Colborne in March of 2002 the **CSL TADOUSSAC** was pushed away from her dock when her forward mooring lines parted. This ship's bow was swung outwards, away from the dock with the stern held fast by the stern anchor.

Shortly following this, the **CSL TADOUSSAC** was towed to Toledo for rudder repairs which required dry docking. The **CSL TADOUSSAC** arrived there on March 27th, under tow of the **JOHN SPENCE** and was taken to the Toledo Shipyard for repairs. Repairs lasted until April 11, 2002 when this ship returned to active service.

On September 5, 2005 the **CSL TADOUSSAC** arrived at Essexville to unload cement clinker at the Essroc Terminal. While extending its boom over the side of the vessel the brakes failed and the structure crashed to the dock. No injuries were reported.

The **CSL TADOUSSAC** can carry up to 30,050 gross tons of cargo per trip, but this is reduced when transiting the St. Lawrence Seaway to 26,800 gross tons. This ship is powered by a 9,600 brake horsepower Sulzer Diesel engine turning a single propeller, giving a speed of 17 miles per hour.

As of the 2008 shipping season the **CSL TADOUSSAC** remains in active service for the CSL fleet. It is one of only three ships in service for this firm which were originally built during the 1960s, the other two being the **HALIFAX**, and **FRONTENAC (5)**. The operational life of this ship was extended by its rebuilding at the beginning of this century and it should remain in active service for several more seasons.

*The stern layout of the **CSL TADOUSSAC** is unique in a number of ways, including the obvious complexity of the unloading gear.. The stern mounting of an unloading boom was unique when this ship was built in 1969. Also of note is the twin smokestacks installed on this ship. The stack markings consist of an orange base, a white band, being topped with a black band.*

CHARLES M. BEEGHLY

In 1957, the American Ship Building Company received a contract worth 8 million dollars to construct a new lake freighter for the Shenango fleet. This fleet was created in 1906 and had in its early years operated some of the largest ships on the Great Lakes. This new ship was to be the first built for the Shenango fleet since the construction of the **WILLIAM P. SNYDER, Jr.** in 1912.

The new vessel was constructed at American Ship Building's Toledo Yard and was launched on November 22, 1958. This 710 foot freighter was one of three nearly identical ships built by American Ship Building, the other two being the **GEORGE M. HUMPHREY (2)**, and **JOHN SHERWIN**. The former ship was built at Lorain for the National Steel Corporation, while the latter was built at Toledo being consigned for the Interlake Steamship fleet.

Following successful sea trials in mid-April, this ship was christened as the **SHENANGO II** on May 16, 1959. This ship's hull was painted in Shenango's dark green color scheme, with its naming reflecting the retirement of the original steamer **SHENANGO** which had been sold out of the fleet in 1958.

On September 29, 1960, the **SHENANGO II** collided with the **CHICAGO TRIBUNE** in the St. Clair River near Marysville, Michigan. The **SHENANGO II** ran aground as a result of this accident requiring tug assistance to be freed, which occurred later the same day.

While in service for Shenango this ship was active in the hauling of ore from the upper lakes to unloading facilities on the lower lakes. While this trade pattern was the most common type of voyage for the **SHENANGO II**, it is noted that she did occasionally carry grain and did transit the St. Lawrence Seaway on occasion.

By 1967, the **SHENANGO II** was considered to excess capacity by Shenango fleet executives and it was sold to the Interlake Steamship Company. Vessel operations by the Shenango fleet continued to wind down following this transaction, and by 1969 it was dissolved following the sale of its last vessel.

Interlake renamed this ship **CHARLES M. BEEGHLY** following its purchase, and placed it into the ore trade. On May 16, 1971, this ship set a ore tonnage record at Huron, Ohio when she arrived with 25,809 gross tons of pellets which had been loaded at Taconite Harbor.

At the end of her 1971 season the **CHARLES M. BEEGHLY** arrived at the Fraser Shipyards at Superior, Wisconsin to be lengthened by 96 feet. This work was done over the winter and increased her length to 806 feet, making her one of the largest ships on the Great Lakes, being eclipsed only by the **ROGER BLOUGH**, and **STEWART J. CORT** which were to make their maiden trips in 1972.

To extend this ship's length it was cut apart in dry dock between its number 3 and 4 cargo holds. Into this was placed a 96 foot section which then became cargo hold 4, with the old number 4 hold becoming number 5. The initial cut was accomplished by December 30, 1971. This modification increased the **BEEGHLY**'s ore hauling capacity by 30% to 32,500 gross tons.

The **BEEGHLY** re-entered service on May 27, 1972, and continued active service in the ore trades, although she was now unable to operate any further east then Lake Erie as her size now prevented her passage through the Welland Canal. Since most of this ship's tonnage commitments had not involved passage through the Seaway this was of little concern. During the 1972-73 winter lay-up, the **BEEGHLY**'s sister ship, **JOHN SHERWIN** was also lengthened to 806 feet at the Fraser Shipyards.

The CHARLES M. BEEGHLY is downbound under the Blue Water Bridge in 1993. She is bound for Rouge Steel, just south of Detroit, Michigan.

The CHARLES M. BEEGHLY is shown downbound at Port Huron, Michigan in 2000. This ship is one of three nearly identical ships built during the 1950s, the others being the GEORGE M. HUMPRHEY (2), and JOHN SHERWIN. Of these, only this ship remains operational as of 2008.

On January 26, 1978 the **CHARLES M. BEEGHLY** ran aground in the St. Marys River. The hull was punctured in this incident and the steamer later went to the Fraser Shipyards at Superior where she was repaired and back in service in May of 1978.

The 1978 season was to be memorable for this ship, as she was involved in a more serious incident later that year. While departing Duluth Harbor on December 22, 1978, the **CHARLES M. BEEGHLY** collided with the north pier of the Duluth Ship Canal holing the starboard side of her hull. Seriously damaged, the crew of the **BEEGHLY** was able to return to Duluth Harbor before it settled on the bottom. The following day, the United States Coast Guard Cutter **MESQUITE**, along with two tugs, were able to raise the **CHARLES M. BEEGHLY** from the bottom, being taken to Fraser Shipyards for extensive repairs.

By the early 1980s many ships being built during the 1950s were being converted into self-unloaders in a bid to improve efficiency in order remain economically viable units. In 1981, the **CHARLES M. BEEGHLY** underwent its second major reconstruction when it arrived at the Fraser Shipyards to be converted into a self-unloader. The **BEEHGLY**'s near twin **JOHN SHERWIN** did not receive such a conversion and has been idle since November 16, 1981. During the 1980s, many ship were idled by the hard economic conditions being experienced by the domestic steel industry in the United States. The **CHARLES M. BEEGHLY** would be idle from late 1982 to 1984. As will be seen, the first trip upon re-entering service in 1984 would turn out to be eventful.

*The forward cabins of the **CHARLES M. BEEGHLY** definitely represent 1950s era shipbuilding practices. Nearly all American ships built during this decade can trace parts of their design to Inland Steel's **WILFRED SYKES** which was launched in 1949, heralding the beginning of the post war shipbuilding boom.*

While departing Superior with a load of taconite pellets on April 27, 1984, the **CHARLES M. BEEGHLY** became caught in strong currents which pushed this ship's stern into the northwest pier of the Superior Ship Canal. The **BEEGHLY**'s stern was holed above the waterline, and the current pushed the bow around, nearly striking the southeast pier being held off only by submerged rocks. Following five hours of effort tugs were able to release the **BEEGHLY**, and she was taken to the Port Terminal at Duluth for damage survey. Reportedly, damages to the ship amounted to approximately $50,000, with $25,000 in damages being inflicted to the pier structures. Repairs were later completed at the Fraser Shipyards, these being completed on May 14, 1984.

Also in 1984, the **CHARLES M. BEEGHLY** became the largest ship to transit the Calumet River near Chicago, Illinois. She again made the news on May 16, 1987 when this steamer became the largest ship to transit up the Black River at Lorain, Ohio with cargo. On this occasion the **BEEGHLY** was loaded with stone.

On June 18, 1994 the **CHARLES M. BEEGHLY** lost a propeller blade while upbound on Whitefish Bay. A return to Sault Ste. Marie was necessary, where it was found that the blade had caused some minor damage to some stern hull plates, requiring a trip to Fraser Shipyards for repairs.

*A stern view of the **CHARLES M. BEEGHLY** illustrates the curved lines of the steamer's design.*

*The **CHARLES M. BEEGHLY** is downbound with ore on September 11, 2005 at St. Clair, Michigan.*

The **CHARLES M. BEEGHLY** was the first ship through the Soo Locks of the 1999 shipping season when she locked through on March 24, 1999.

This steamer ran aground in the Detroit River on October 4, 2001 near Belle Isle. The **CHARLES M. BEEGHLY** was downbound at the time, and was freed with the assistance of the **JOYCE L. VAN ENKEVORT** with no reported damages.

While in winter lay-up at Sturgeon Bay in March of 2007, this ship's name was painted out and replaced by **JAMES A. OBERSTAR** in honor of a Minnesota congressman with a long history of advocating Great Lakes related programs. This renaming was to be brief as this ship was renamed back to **CHARLES M. BEEGHLY** a short time later, without ever operating as the **JAMES A. OBERSTAR**.

This steamer is powered by a General Electric steam turbine capable of generating 9,350 shaft horsepower. With this power plant this ship can reach speeds up to 17 miles per hour.

The **CHARLES M. BEEGHLY** can carry up to 31,000 gross tons of cargo, which is loaded into the ship through 25 hatches each measuring 48 feet long by 11 feet long. The main cargoes hauled by this steamer are ore, coal, and stones and is unloaded onto shore by a 250 foot stern mounted unloading boom.

The **CHARLES M. BEEGHLY** became the largest operating steamer on the Great Lakes, following the repowering to diesel of the **LEE A. TREGURTHA** in 2006. The **CHARLES M. BEEGHLY** is scheduled to be repowered at the end of the 2008 season with 2 Bergen diesel engines.

On August 27, 2008, Interlake Steamship announced that the **JOHN SHERWIN** would be converted into a self-unloader, and repowered to diesel at Bay Shipbuilding, following her nearly three decades of inactivity. She is scheduled to rejoin her sister ship, **CHARLES M. BEEGHLY**, in active service during the 2010 season.

As of the 2008 shipping season, the **CHARLES M. BEEGHLY** remains hard at work serving its owners needs in the transportation of raw materials. A common destination being the Rouge River where she hauls ore into the Severstal Steel Plant. The lengthening, self-unloading conversion, along with the upcoming repowering will ensure that this ship remains a viable carrier in the future.

*The **CHARLES M. BEEGHLY** is downbound on the St. Clair River on November 17, 2007.*

QUICK REFERENCE GUIDE

YANKCANUCK (2)-Built: 1963-Collingwood Shipyards, Collingwood, Ontario. Dimensions: 324'3" x 49' x 26'. Operator: Purvis Marine Limited. Official Number: 318683

PATHFINDER (3)-Built: 1953-Great Lakes Engineering Works, River Rouge, Michigan. Dimensions: 606'2" x 70' x 36'. Launched as J. L. MAUTHE. Converted into a self-unloading barge and renamed PATHFINDER (3) in 1998. Operator: Interlake Steamship Company. Official Number: 264738

CANADIAN LEADER-Built: 1967-Collingwood Shipyards, Collingwood, Ontario. Dimensions: 730' x 75' x 39'8". Launched as FEUX-FOLLETS, renamed CANADIAN LEADER in 1972. Operator: Seaway Marine Transport Official Number: 325746

LEWIS J. KUBER-Built: 1952-Bethlehem Steel Shipbuilding Division, Sparrows Point, Maryland. Dimensions: 616' 10" x 70' x 37'. Launched as SPARROWS POINT, renamed BUCKEYE in 1991, renamed LEWIS J. KUBER in 2006. Lengthened 72' in 1958. Converted into a self-unloader in 1980. Converted into a barge in 2006. Operator-VanEnkevort Tug & Barge. Official Number: 264391

ALGOEAST-Built: 1977-Mitsubishi Heavy Industries, Shimonoseki, Japan. Dimensions: 431' 5" x 65' 7" x 35' 5". Launched as TEXACO BRAVE, renamed LE BRAVE in 1986, renamed IMPERIAL ST. LAWRENCE in 1997, renamed ALGOEAST in 1998. Operator: Algoma Tankers. Official Number: 371941

ROGER BLOUGH-Built: 1972-American Ship Building Company, Lorain, Ohio. Dimensions: 858' x 105' x 41' 6". Operator: Great Lakes Fleet, Inc. Official Number: 533062

JOHN B. AIRD-Built: 1983-Collingwood Shipyards, Collingwood, Ontario. Dimensions: 730' x 76' 1" x 46' 6". Operator-Seaway Marine Transport. Official Number: 802923

PAUL R. TREGURTHA-Built: 1981-American Ship Building Company, Lorain, Ohio, Dimensions: 1013' 6" x 105' x 56'. Launched as WILLIAM J. DELANCEY, renamed PAUL R. TREGURTHA in 1990. Operator: Interlake Steamship. Official Number: 631668

MARITIME TRADER-Built: 1967-Collingwood Shipyards, Collingwood, Ontario. Dimensions: 607' 10" x 62' x 36'. Launched as MANTADOC, renamed TEAKGLEN in 2002, renamed MARITIME TRADER in 2005. Operator: Voyageur Marine. Official Number: 325744

JOHN G. MUNSON (2)-Built: 1952-Manitowoc Shipbuilding, Manitowoc, Wisconsin. Dimensions: 768' 3" x 72' x 36'. Lengthened 102' in 1976. Operator: Great Lakes Fleet, Inc. Official Number: 264136

ALGOWAY (2)-Built: 1972-Collingwood Shipyards, Collingwood, Ontario. Dimensions: 650' x 72' x 40'. Operator–Seaway Marine Transport. Official Number: 331090.

J. A. W. IGLEHART-Built: 1936-Sun Shipbuilding, Chester, Pennsylvania. Dimensions: 501' 6" x 68' 03 x 37'. Launched as PAN AMOCO, renamed AMOCO in 1955, renamed H. R. SCHEMN in 1960, renamed J. A. W. IGLEHART in 1965. Launched as tanker, converted into cement carrier in 1965. Operator: Inland Lakes Management. Official Number: 235570

ROBERT S. PIERSON (2)-Built: 1974-American Ship Building Company, Lorain, Ohio. Dimensions: 630' x 68' x 36' 11". Launched as WOLVERINE, renamed ROBERT S. PIERSON in 2008. Operator: Lower Lakes Towing. Official Number: 832253

MAUMEE-Built: 1929-American Ship Building Company, Lorain, Ohio. Dimensions: 604' 9" x 60' x 32'. Launched as WILLIAM G. CLYDE, renamed CALCITE II in 1961, renamed MAUMEE in 2001. Converted into a self-unloader in 1961. Operator: Grand River Navigation. Official Number: 228886

HALIFAX-Built: 1963-Davie Shipbuilding, Lauzon, Quebec. Dimensions: 730' 2" x 75' x 39' 3". Launched as FRANKCLIFFE HALL, renamed HALIFAX in 1988. Converted into a self-unloader and deepened by 6' in 1980. Operator: Canada Steamship Lines. Official Number: 313963

AMERICAN VALOR-Built: 1953-American Ship Building Company, Lorain, Ohio. Dimensions: 767' x 70' x 36'. Launched as ARMCO, renamed AMERICAN VALOR in 2006. Lengthened 120' in 1974. Converted into a self-unloader in 1982. Operator: American Steamship Company. Official Number: 265621

JAMES NORRIS-Built: 1952-Midland Shipyards, Midland, Ontario. Dimensions: 663' 6" x 67' x 35'. Converted into a self-unloader in 1981. Operator: Seaway Marine Transport. Official Number: 178247

WALTER J. McCARTHY, JR.-Built: 1977-Bay Shipbuilding, Sturgeon Bay, Wisconsin. Dimensions: 1000' x 105' x 56'. Launched as BELLE RIVER, renamed WALTER J. McCARTHY, JR. in 1990. Operator: American Steamship Company. Official Number: 585952

CSL TADOUSSAC-Built: 1969-Collingwood Shipyards, Collingwood, Ontario. Dimensions: 730' x 78' x 42'. Launched as TADOUSSAC, renamed CSL TADOUSSAC in 2001. Widened by 3' in 2001. Operator: Canada Steamship Lines. Official Number: 325750

CHARLES M. BEEGHLY-Built: 1959-American Ship Building Company, Toledo, Ohio. Dimensions: 806' x 75' x 37' 06". Launched as SHENANGO II, renamed CHARLES M. BEEGHLY in 1967. Lengthened 96' in 1972. Converted into a self-unloader in 1981. Operator: Interlake Steamship. Official Number: 278807

VESSEL INDEX

A
AFFLECK, B.F. 83
AGAWA CANYON 49, 52
AIRD, JOHN B. 30-33
ALGOBAY 32
ALGOEAST 20-23
ALGOMARINE 72
ALGOPORT 32
ALGORAIL(2) 49, 51
ALGOSOO(2) 28
ALGOSTEEL(2) 72
ALGOWAY(2) 4, 50-52
ALGOWOOD 32
ALPENA(2) 55, 57
AMERICAN CENTURY 85
AMERICAN INTEGRITY 85
AMERICAN REPUBLIC 36
AMERICAN SPIRIT 36
AMERICAN VALOR 73, 75-77
AMHERSTBURG 55
AMOCO 53, 57
ANDERSON, ARTHUR M. 6, 47, 60
ANDRIE, MARY BETH 58
ANGLIAN LADY 3, 13
APPOLONIA 68
ARMCO 73-76
AVENGER IV 13, 17, 40, 70, 83

B
BARBER, E.B. 30
BARKER, JAMES R. 34, 36, 38
BEAVERCLIFFE HALL 68
BEEGHLY, CHARLES M. 36, 93-97
BELLE RIVER 38, 83-85
BLOUGH, ROGER 24-29, 47, 87, 93
BOARDMAN, JOHN W. 53
BOLAND, JOHN J.(3) 45, 47, 75
BRADLEY, CARL D.(2) 45
BUCKEYE(3) 16-19
BURNS HARBOR 17, 85
BUSCH, GREGORY J. 63

C
CALCITE 63
CALCITE II 63-65
CALLOWAY, CASON J. 6, 47
CALUMET(3) 67
CANADIAN ENTERPRISE 38
CANADIAN EXPLORER 80
CANADIAN LEADER 11-14, 82
CANADIAN PROVIDER 11, 82
CANADIAN TRANSFER 80
CARNAHAN, PAUL H. 55
CASTLE, LEWIS 90
CEDARGLEN(2) 72
CHICAGO TRIBUNE 93
CHIEF WAWATAM 3
CLARKE, PHILIP R. 6, 26, 47, 73
CLYDE, WILLIAM G. 63
COHEN, WILFRED M. 13, 17, 30
COLUMBIA STAR 34, 73
CORT, STEWART J. 17, 24, 26, 28, 93
COVERDALE 78
CRAPO, S.T. 57
CRESWELL, PETER R. 32
CSL TADOUSSAC 88, 90-92

D
DAVID Z. 62
DeCHAMPLAIN, SAMUEL 57
DELANCEY, WILLIAM J. 34, 36
DESGAGNES, ROLAND 68
DESMARAIS, LOUIS R. 88
DETROIT EDISON(2) 45, 47
DOROTHY ANN 8, 10
DUC D'ORLEANS 59
DUNN, SIR JAMES 78

E
EARL W. 62
EASTERN SHELL 83
ENGLISH RIVER 55

VESSEL INDEX

F
FERBERT, A.H. 26
FEUX FOLLETS 11
FITZGERALD, EDMUND 28, 73
FORD, E.M. 57
FORD, J.B. 57
FOY, LEWIS WILSON 17
FRANKCLIFFE HALL(1) 68
FRANKCLIFFE HALL(2) 68, 70
FRONTENAC(5) 68, 72, 92

G
GLENADA 85
GLENN, ALEXANDER SIR 88
GLOXINIA 68
GOTT, EDWIN H. 26, 28, 85
GRAMPA WOO 85

H
HALIFAX 68-72, 92
HAMILTON TRANSFER 80
HERBERT A 78
HILLMAN, J.H. JR. 80
HOCHELAGA 78
HOEY, PATRICIA 65, 90
HOYT, ELTON 2ND 6, 15
HUMPHREY, GEORGE M.(2) 93-94

I
IGLEHART, J.A.W. 53-57
ILLINOIS 90
IMPERIAL ST. LAWRENCE(2) 20-21
INDIANA HARBOR 85
INNOVATION 57
INTEGRITY 57
IOWA 70

J
JACKLYN M. 57
JACKMAN, CAPT. HENRY 32
JODREY, ROY A. 49
JOHNSTOWN 15, 17

K
KATMAI BAY 70
KELLERS, FREDERICK T. 63
KINSMAN INDEPENDENT(3) 44
KUBER, JAMES L. 75
KUBER, LEWIS J. 15, 19
KYES, ROGER M. 58

L
L.D., FRANCOIS 40
LAWRENCECLIFFE HALL 68
LE BRAVE 20
LEECLIFFE HALL 68
LEITCH, GORDON C.(1) 78
LEON FRASER 57
LOWSON, SIR DENYS 40, 42

M
MAINE 17
MALABAR VI 63
MANITOU 51
MANITOULIN(5) 45, 88
MANTADOC(2) 40-42
MAPLECLIFFE HALL 68
MARIPOSA 73
MARITIME TRADER 40, 42-44
MAUMEE 63, 65-67
MAUTHE, J.L. 5-9
McCARTHY, WALTER J. JR. 38-39, 83-87
McKEIL, EVANS 40
McLEAN, JOHN 30
MENASHA 51, 90
MESABI MINER 34, 36
MESQUITE 95
MIDDLETOWN 17
MISSOURI 17, 70
MITCHELL, SAMUEL 53
MOBILE BAY 70
MOMS MONEY 63
MONTREALAIS 82
MOORE, OLIVE L. 19
MUNSON, JOHN G.(2) 45-48
MURRAY BAY 36

VESSEL INDEX

N
NANCY K. 13
NANTICOKE 88
NORRIS, JAMES 78-82
NORTHCLIFFE HALL 68
NORTON, DAVID Z.(3) 60

O
OBERSTAR, JAMES A. 97
OGLEBAY, CRISPIN(2) 80
OGLEBAY, EARL W. 60
OHIO 70
OLDS, IRVING S. 73, 75
OREGON 65
OTTERCLIFFE HALL 68

P
PAN-AMOCO 53
PARISIEN, JEAN 88
PATHFINDER(3) 6, 8-10
PENNISULA 83
PENNSYLVANIA 55, 90
PIERSON, ROBERT S.(2) 58, 62
PRESQUE ISLE(2) 47
PURVIS, JOHN 8, 65

Q
QUEBECOIS 82

R
RESERVE 60, 73, 75
ROBINSON BAY 90
ROESCH, WILLIAM R. 58

S
SASKATCHEWAN PIONEER 44
SCHEMM, HR 53
SEAWAY QUEEN 78
SHANNON 51, 90
SHENANGO 93
SHENANGO II 93
SHERMAN, FRANK A. 78
SHERWIN, JOHN 93-95
SLOAN, GEORGE A. 63, 65
SNYDER, WILLIAM P. JR. 93
SOLTA 70

S *(CONT'D)*
SPARROWS POINT 15-17
SPEER, EDGAR B. 26, 28, 38
SPENCE, JOHN 92
ST. CLAIR(2) 83
ST. LAWRENCE(2) 49
ST. MARYS CHALLENGER 57
STADACONA(3) 78
STAHL, ROGER 51, 55
STEELTON(2) 15
STINSON, GEORGE A. 36
STORMONT 65
SYKES, WILFRED 95

T
TADOUSSAC(4) 88-90
TARANTAU 88
TAYLOR, MYRON C. 65
TEAKGLEN 42, 43
TEXACO BRAVE(2) 20
THAYER, PAUL 58, 60
THUNDER BAY(2) 78
THUNDER CAPE 83
TREGURTHA, LEE A. 97
TREGURTHA, PAUL R. 34-39

U
USCG MACKINAW 47

V
VANDOC(2) 42
VAN ENKEVORT, JOYCE L. 97
VERMONT 55
VICTORY 19
VOYAGEUR INDEPENDENT 44
VOYAGEUR PIONEER 44

W
WESTFORT 85
WOLVERINE(4) 58-62
WYOMING 55, 72, 90

Y
YANKCANUCK(1) 1
YANKCANUCK(2) 1-5

www.ingramcontent.com/pod-product-compliance
Lightning Source LLC
Chambersburg PA
CBHW080521110426
42742CB00017B/3194